Rooted & Radiant

Faith-Filled Devotional for the Social Introvert Entrepreneur

Rooted & Radiant

© 2025 Janet Bablo. All rights reserved.

Published by J Eagle Agency Publishing, an imprint of J Eagle Agency

New York, USA

ISBN (Paperback): [979-8-9932543-0-2]

No part of this book may be reproduced, stored in a retrieval system, or transmitted in any form or by any means, electronic, mechanical, photocopying, recording, or otherwise, without prior written permission of the publisher, except for brief quotations in critical articles or reviews.

Scripture quotations marked NLT are from the Holy Bible, New Living Translation, © 1996, 2004, 2015 by Tyndale House Foundation. Used by permission of Tyndale House Publishers, Inc. All rights reserved. Scripture quotations marked NIV are from the Holy Bible, New International Version®, NIV®, © 1973, 1978, 1984, 2011 by Biblica, Inc.™ Used by permission. All rights reserved worldwide. Scripture quotations marked AMPC are from the Amplified Bible, Classic Edition, © 1954, 1958, 1962, 1964, 1965, 1987 by The Lockman Foundation. Used by permission. All rights reserved. Scripture quotations marked NKJV are from the New King James Version®, © 1982 by Thomas Nelson. Used by permission. All rights reserved.

Printed in the United States of America

Dedication

To the Holy Spirit, my greatest Helper and Friend,

the One who guided me on the journey to discovery,

who reminds me of who I am in every aspect of life; spiritually, emotionally, mentally, and even as an entrepreneur.

This book would not exist without His presence, counsel, and power.

And to every social introvert entrepreneur learning to live

rooted in Christ and radiant in purpose.

This devotional is for you.

Acknowledgements

First, I acknowledge my Lord and Savior, Jesus Christ, and the precious Holy Spirit, who has been my Counselor, Teacher, and Companion. Without His guidance, there would be no vision, no discovery, and no book in your hands today.

To Bishop David Oyedepo – The Lion. The Eagle. My Papa. A Father in the Faith. You are my "OG" teacher, the vessel through whom the Lord first sparked what is now manifesting within me. Your words have been a constant guide, making the baby in my belly leap with purpose and understanding. The seeds you planted continue to grow, and I am forever grateful to walk this journey as your student. Thank you, Papa. Truly, Eagle no dey born chicken.

I am also deeply grateful to Dr. Myles Munroe, whose timeless wisdom on vision and purpose guides me; Pastor Touré Roberts, whose teachings came at a very low point, reminding me that God's plan was still intact; Prophet & Psalmist Dunsin Oyekan, my teacher, whose sound and teachings have carried me into encounters with God's presence; and Apostle Joshua Selman, from whom I have learned mysteries of the Kingdom, wisdom for living, the way of honor, and many treasures of truth that have reshaped my walk with God."

To my parents, Taiwo & David, thank you for being the first vessels through whom God's love and wisdom were made real to me. Your prayers and sacrifices laid the foundation for everything I am becoming. I celebrate you, honor you, and carry your legacy forward.

To my family, close friends, and my pastors, Dr. Adebisi & Abby Oyesile, thank you for your love, prayers, encouragement, support, and spiritual guidance. Your faithfulness has shaped my walk, and I am forever grateful.

To my NSN family (Nighttime Spiritual Nutrition), thank you for the years of fellowship, consistency, and hunger for God's Word. We have studied Genesis to Revelation year after year, and your devotion has sharpened me, strengthened me, and kept my spirit anchored. I honor you, and I am grateful for the community we have built together.

Finally, to every social introvert entrepreneur who picks up this devotional: I acknowledge you. You are seen. You are not alone. May you find in these pages the strength to be rooted in Christ and radiant in purpose.

Table of Contents

- Dedication iii
- Acknowledgements iv
- Table of Contents .... v–vi
- Introduction vii

Part One: Foundations

1. Who Is the Social Introvert Entrepreneur? 2
2. God's Purpose in Personality 11
3. Entrepreneurship as Kingdom Assignment 18

Part Two: The 30-Day Devotional Journey

Section 1: Identity & Design

- Day 1: Fearfully & Wonderfully Made............................. 27
- Day 2: Seasons of Silence & Speech 30
- Day 3: Jesus, Our Pattern of Balance 33
- Day 4: The Gift of Stillness.. 36
- Day 5: Purpose Precedes Personality 39
- Day 6: The Spirit of Boldness & Love 42

Section 2: Grace for Both Worlds

- Day 7: Rest for the Weary 46
- Day 8: The Ministry of Presence 49
- Day 9: Chosen for the Inner Circle.................................. 52
- Day 10: Authenticity Opens Doors.................................. 55
- Day 11: In Quietness is Strength 58
- Day 12: God Rejoices Over You 61

Section 3: Boldness in Business

- Day 13: Occupy Till I Come 65
- Day 14: Wisdom Builds the House 68
- Day 15: Do Business God's Way 71
- Day 16: Speaking with Grace & Truth 74
- Day 17: Faith Over Fear in Leadership 77
- Day 18: Diligence Brings Influence 80

Section 4: Rest & Recharge

- Day 19: Abide in the Vine 84
- Day 20: Elijah by the Brook 87
- Day 21: The Gift of Sleep & Renewal 90
- Day 22: Peace That Guards You 93
- Day 23: Strength in Stillness.. 96
- Day 24: The Shepherd Restores My Soul 99

Section 5: Community & Boundaries

- Day 25: Iron Sharpens Iron 103
- Day 26: Guard Your Heart 106
- Day 27: The Body Needs Every Part 109

Section 6: Prophetic Precision & Vision

- Day 28: Write the Vision 113
- Day 29: Times & Seasons 116
- Day 30: Finish Strong 119

Closing Word

- Go and shine 122
- Prayer for You 123
- Personal Notes (Your Journey Entry).. 124

Introduction

When God first began to stir this book in my heart, I was searching for resources that spoke to who I am: a believer, an entrepreneur, and a social introvert. There are many books for leaders, many devotionals for Christians, and even materials for introverts in business, but very few that combine all three. I realized that part of my assignment was to write what I could not find.

This devotional is not about labeling yourself but about discovering how God's intentional design works through you. Your personality is not your identity, you are first and foremost a child of God, loved and chosen. But your personality is part of the equipment He gave you to walk out your Kingdom assignment. For social introverts, this means learning to value both our capacity for connection and our deep need for solitude.

The book is divided into two parts. Part One lays the foundation. In three chapters, we will explore who the social introvert entrepreneur is, what God says about personality and purpose, and how entrepreneurship itself is a Kingdom assignment. This teaching will root you in biblical truth and give you language for your design.

Part Two is a 30-day devotional journey. Each day includes scripture, reflection, prayers, and declarations. It is meant to be read slowly, one day at a time. Don't rush. Let the Word sink deep into your heart. Pause for the Reflection Questions. Pray the prayers aloud. Make the declarations boldly. Use the journaling space to capture what God speaks to you.

As you journey through these pages, my prayer is that you will become both rooted and radiant; rooted in Christ and radiant with His wisdom, creativity, and strength. May you come to see your personality not as a limitation, but as a Kingdom strategy. And may every part of who you are shine for the glory of God.

I begin in the name of the Father, the Son, and the Holy Spirit. Amen!

PART ONE: FOUNDATIONS

Chapter 1: Who Is the Social Introvert Entrepreneur?

Outline

- The four types of introverts (Jonathan Cheek's framework: social, thinking, anxious, restrained).
- Focus on the "social introvert."
- How this personality is both social and rooted in solitude.
- Jesus as the model: engaging crowds but retreating to pray (Luke 5:16).
- Why this design is powerful for entrepreneurship.

The Many Faces of Introversion

For years, people have misunderstood introverts. If you're quiet, they assume you're shy. If you leave early from a gathering, they think you're antisocial. And if you are social, they immediately assume you must be an extrovert. But introversion is not that simple.

Psychologist Jonathan Cheek and his colleagues discovered that there isn't just one kind of introvert. In fact, they identified four types:

1. Social Introverts - They enjoy being with people, but not everywhere and not all the time. They'd rather spend hours in deep conversation with a few than be lost in a sea of many.
2. Thinking Introverts - They live deeply in their thoughts. Reflection, creativity, and imagination fuel them.
3. Anxious Introverts - They struggle with self-consciousness and can feel uneasy in groups, replaying what they said long after the moment has passed.
4. Restrained Introverts - They move slowly and deliberately. They warm up on their own terms, often observing before stepping in.

This framework gives us helpful language for understanding personality. However, our foundation is always the Word of God, which reminds us that identity and design ultimately come from Him.

You see, introverts are not one-dimensional. And this devotional is written with a very specific kind in mind: the social introvert. Understanding these differences matters because many of us have been mislabeled. You may have been told you are "too much" when you're social, or "too quiet" when you step back. Yet Scripture reminds us in Psalm 139:14 (NKJV):

"I will praise You, for I am fearfully and wonderfully made; marvelous are Your works, and that my soul knows very well."

Your wiring is not an accident. It is God's workmanship.

The Social Introvert Explained

A social introvert doesn't hide from people; they actually like them. They can lead, laugh, and even light up a stage when the moment calls for it. But here's the key: when the moment is over, they need to step back, recharge, and be alone with their thought and with God. This is not weakness. This is rhythm. This is design.

This rhythm is often misunderstood. Extroverts may keep going long after you've withdrawn, while anxious introverts may avoid the event entirely. But the social introvert is unique: you can step forward with confidence and step back with peace. As a social introvert entrepreneur, you might feel tension sometimes. On one hand, you know how to network, host, and lead. On the other, you treasure silence, reflection, and rest. But the beauty is, you were never meant to choose one over the other. God gave you the capacity for both.

For me, this dual rhythm shows up in ways that sometimes surprise people. I can meet someone today and they encounter Janet the talker, super expressive, animated, and fully present in the conversation. Then I meet someone tomorrow and suddenly I'm nicknamed "Gentle J", quiet, soft-spoken, and content to simply observe. Which one is the "real me"? Both. That's the paradox and the gift of the social introvert.

This is why social introverts can thrive as entrepreneurs. They can stand before investors, pitch with clarity, or lead teams with charisma. But they're also wise enough to pause, process, and seek God before the next step.

"Be still, and know that I am God..." - Psalm 46:10a (NKJV)

Stillness is not your escape. It is your empowerment. It is in the quiet, when others assume you have withdrawn, that God whispers strategy, renews your energy, and anchors your purpose.

Jesus as the Model

The ultimate picture of the social introvert rhythm is found in Jesus Himself. He was deeply social. He taught multitudes on hillsides, dined with tax collectors and sinners, and let children climb onto His lap. He healed the sick and comforted the broken. He could sit at a wedding feast and turn water into wine or spend hours healing every person who was brought to Him. Jesus was deeply social, approachable, magnetic; people wanted to be near Him.

And yet, He also protected His solitude. The Gospels show us repeatedly that after moments of intense ministry, Jesus withdrew to be alone with His Father.

"And when He had sent the multitudes away, He went up on the mountain by Himself to pray. Now when evening came, He was alone there." - Matthew 14:23 (NKJV)

"Now in the morning, having risen a long while before daylight, He went out and departed to a solitary place; and there He prayed." - Mark 1:35 (NKJV)

"And He withdrew from them about a stone's throw, and He knelt down and prayed." - Luke 22:41 (NKJV)

Notice the rhythm: connection, then withdrawal; engagement, then solitude. Jesus knew when to pour out and when to pull back. This is the life of a social introvert. You can step forward when God calls you into a room, but you also know when to step away into prayer. Both are necessary.

Jesus as the Model (Expanded with prayer & fasting)

When Jesus withdrew, it wasn't because He was weak or because He didn't enjoy people. It was because He understood that His power flowed from His Father. The miracles, the wisdom, the boldness in public, all of it was fueled by His hidden life of prayer. This is where many people misunderstand introverts. They think stepping back means something is wrong. But for the social introvert, retreat is not avoidance, it's alignment. Just as Jesus pulled away to be re-centered, you too need solitude to be refilled with strength, clarity, and vision.

The secret of Jesus' ministry wasn't just His public teaching; it was His private communion. The crowds saw the power, but the Father saw the surrender. And it was the surrender that birthed the power. That surrender often came through prayer and fasting. Before launching His public ministry, Jesus fasted forty days in the wilderness (Luke 4:1-2). Before choosing His twelve disciples, He spent the night in prayer (Luke 6:12-13). His rhythm of engaging people always flowed from deeper encounters with the Father in hidden places.

So, when you feel the need to step back after pouring out, whether that's after leading a team, closing a deal, or ministering in your business; remember you are not withdrawing in weakness. You're following Jesus' example.

Your solitude is not empty. It is sacred. It is the well from which your public life draws living water. And just as Jesus strengthened Himself through prayer and fasting, you too can sustain your assignment by anchoring every season of visibility in rhythms of intimacy with God.

The Gospels show us that Jesus' rhythm of solitude was consistent, not occasional. He did not wait until He was burned out to pray. Prayer and fasting were built into His life from the beginning.

"Now in the morning, having risen a long while before daylight, He went out and departed to a solitary place; and there He prayed." - Mark 1:35 (NKJV)

"And He withdrew from them about a stone's throw, and He knelt down and prayed." - Luke 22:41 (NKJV)

Before every major decision, Jesus prayed. Before stepping into public ministry, He fasted. Before enduring the cross, He knelt in Gethsemane. For the social introvert entrepreneur, this is a vital reminder: your private rhythm sustains your public assignment. It's not enough to be gifted in conversation, charismatic in meetings, or strategic in planning. Without the secret place, your influence will run dry.

Prayer anchors you. Fasting sharpens you. Solitude refills you. These practices don't make you weaker or lazy in business; they make you unshakable.

Why This Design Is Powerful for Entrepreneurship

The business world often glorifies the extrovert; the person who never stops talking, the tireless networker, always-available leader. But in reality, the Kingdom doesn't need replicas. God didn't design everyone to lead that way. It needs originals. He designed social introverts with a balance that is not a weakness but a weapon. As a social introvert, you bring something the world desperately needs.

A social introvert entrepreneur carries the unique strengths that set you apart:

Depth and Discernment - You don't just rush into decisions. You pause, reflect, and seek God before moving forward. That means your decisions carry weight because they have been processed in prayer and thought. This brings stability into your business.

Authenticity in Connection - You don't thrive on shallow small talk; You prefer meaningful interaction. People remember how genuine you are, and that builds long-term trust.

Balance of Visibility and Reflection - You can step forward into visibility when the moment requires it, but you also know when to retreat to reset. That rhythm protects you from burnout and gives you longevity in leadership whether in business or ministry.

Think of it this way: an extrovert might dominate the room, but a social introvert discerns the room. You listen for what's not being said. You notice details others miss. That discernment often becomes the strategy that shifts everything.

I've been in events where everyone's goal is to meet the main act, the star of the night, the one in the spotlight. I don't bother chasing that route because I know that's already everyone's target. Instead, I've learned that kings attract kings. In that same room are other kings, individuals who may not have the limelight, entourages, or heavy protocol, but they carry real weight and influence. Many overlook them because they don't look like kings. Yet these hidden connections are often where God places the true keys to destiny. This is not just networking wisdom; it's a Kingdom truth.

I have been in rooms where I was completely overlooked, until someone who knows me pointed me out. In that moment, people suddenly became curious. Their posture shifted. It wasn't my chasing that created the opening, but God's timing and the testimony of someone else. That's how the Lord works with social introverts: you don't have to push your way in. God has a way of making room for you when it's your time to be seen.

Psalm 1:3 (AMPC) describes the blessed person this way: *"He shall be like a tree firmly planted [and tended] by the streams of water, ready to bring forth its fruit in its season; its leaf also shall not fade or wither; and everything he does shall prosper [and come to maturity]."*

This is your design. Not rushed, not shallow but firmly planted and rooted like a tree, radiant in fruitfulness. Dr. Myles Munroe often said,

"When the purpose of a thing is not known, abuse is inevitable." That truth applies not only to business and leadership, but also to your personality. When you don't understand how God designed you, you may try to force yourself into a mold that was never yours. But when you discover purpose, you realize that even your introversion is a tool in God's hand.

As a social introvert entrepreneur, you must stop seeing yourself as "less than" because you aren't constantly in the spotlight. You were not designed to be available everywhere, all the time. You were designed to move with intentionality, to pour out where God has called you, and to retreat when He says, "be still."

Here's an example: imagine leading a team of ten. An extroverted leader might thrive on constant group meetings and lots of visible energy. But as a social introvert, you may prefer one-on-one check-ins, quiet observation, and thoughtful responses. To some, that may look less energetic, but in reality, it builds deeper trust and stronger loyalty because your team feels genuinely seen and heard.

At the same time, when you must step into meetings with multiple people involved, or when you're responsible for leading across several teams at once, it takes a lot of mental energy. You can do it, and you can even do it well, but it costs you more internally than it might cost an extrovert. That doesn't make you weaker; it simply means you must steward your energy wisely. Your strength is in knowing how to manage that output, so you don't run dry.

This is your Kingdom advantage. Where others scatter their energy everywhere, you focus it where it matters most. Where others may be drained by trying to stay visible, you are refilled by your rhythm of solitude. Purpose is not about being like everyone else. It is about stewarding who God made you to be and then allowing that design to flourish in the assignment He has given you.

Reflection Questions

- What part of the "social introvert" description resonates most with you personally?

- How does Jesus' rhythm of engaging with crowds and then retreating to pray challenge or affirm the way you live?
- Where have you seen your social introversion serve as a strength in leadership, relationships, or business opportunities?

✎. Write your reflections below:

Prayers

Heavenly Father, I thank You that my true identity is as Your child, chosen, loved, and set apart. Nothing about me is by accident. You formed me with care, and even my personality is part of Your intentional design.

Teach me to embrace the way You wired me, not as the world defines me, but as You see me. Where I have misunderstood or resisted my personality, give me grace to see it as a gift. Help me to follow the pattern of Jesus, to pour out when called, but also to retreat into Your presence for strength and renewal.

Lord, may I never confuse my personality with my identity. Keep me rooted in You, and help me to steward my design as a tool for Kingdom purpose. In every assignment, let my confidence come from being Your child first and foremost.

In Jesus' name, Amen.

Declarations

- I decree and declare that I am first and foremost a child of God, deeply loved and intentionally created.
- I decree and declare that my personality is not a mistake but part of God's divine design.
- I decree and declare that I will embrace the way God wired me and steward it faithfully for His Kingdom.
- I decree and declare that I will walk in the balance of solitude and connection, following the example of Jesus.
- I decree and declare that when I step into rooms, my confidence is rooted in God's presence and not in people's perception.
- I decree and declare that I shine with God's wisdom and strength in every assignment given to me.

In Jesus' mighty and matchless name, Amen!

Chapter 2: God's Purpose in Personality

Outline

- God's Intentional Design.
- Purpose precedes personality.
- Every temperament has a divine assignment.
- Introversion as a strategy, not a flaw.
- Living from identity in Christ.

Purpose Precedes Personality

Dr. Myles Munroe often said, "Purpose is the original intent in the mind of God for why something exists." This principle doesn't just apply to nations, leadership, or vision, it also applies to you. Your personality was never an afterthought. It was carefully designed to serve the assignment God placed on your life.

Scripture confirms this order:

God told Jeremiah, *"Before I formed you in the womb, I knew you" (Jeremiah 1:5 NKJV)*. That means Jeremiah's purpose existed before his body, and before his personality, were ever shaped.

David declared, *"All the days ordained for me were written in Your book before one of them came to be" (Psalm 139:16 NIV)*. That means destiny was established before expression.

Your temperament, whether you lean toward introversion, extroversion, or somewhere in between, is tied to the divine assignment God placed on your life.

For example, Moses was hesitant to speak (Exodus 4:10), yet God still called him to deliver Israel. His reflective, cautious nature became a strength for leading such a stubborn people. Peter, on the other hand, was bold and outspoken. His extroverted fire became fuel for the

Church's expansion. Both were chosen. Both were designed with purpose in mind.

This is why comparison is so dangerous. You are not meant to copy the boldness of Peter if God designed you with the steady rhythm of Moses. Nor are you meant to hide in Moses' hesitation if God gave you Peter's fire. Personality is simply the vessel; purpose is the oil. Your social introversion, then, is not a weakness to apologize for but a strategy to embrace. God gave you the ability to engage meaningfully and retreat wisely because your assignment requires both. He knew the kind of entrepreneur, leader, and Kingdom builder you would need to be. When you understand that purpose precedes personality, you stop fighting who you are and start stewarding who you are.

David also declared this truth:

"Your eyes saw my substance, being yet unformed. And in Your book, they all were written, the days fashioned for me, when as yet there were none of them." - Psalm 139:16 (NKJV)

Destiny was written before your personality ever found expression. God first set your assignment, and then He designed your temperament to support it. Throughout scripture, we see how God used different personalities to advance His Kingdom. Peter was fiery, outspoken, and bold, his extroverted passion gave him courage to stand up on the day of Pentecost and preach to thousands. John, however, was relational, tender, and deeply reflective, his writings echo intimacy and love, revealing the heart of Jesus as no one else did.

Paul was structured, disciplined, and uncompromising in truth, perfectly suited to establish doctrine and order for the early Church. Barnabas, on the other hand, was an encourager, patient and gentle, always building others up and drawing them into the work. Both men were vital, though their personalities were radically different. This is why comparison is so dangerous. You were not called to mimic Peter's boldness if God gave you John's tenderness. Nor should you despise your Barnabas-like encouragement if God designed you with Paul's structure. Again, personality is simply the vessel; purpose is the oil.

The truth is this: when you understand that purpose comes first, you stop fighting who you are. You stop apologizing for your rhythm and start stewarding it. Your design is not a mistake; it is divine strategy.

Every Temperament Has a Divine Assignment

God is not limited to one type of person. He delights in using different temperaments to accomplish His will. The way He wired you is not in competition with others, but in collaboration with His Kingdom plan.

Romans 12:6 (NKJV) says, "Having then gifts differing according to the grace that is given to us, let us use them." Grace and gifting are distributed differently, but each is necessary.

Consider how God used distinct personalities throughout the Bible:

Nehemiah - A builder with a practical, strategic mind. His temperament gave him the persistence to rally people and rebuild Jerusalem's walls.

Deborah - A judge and prophetess whose confidence and wisdom inspired a nation. Her temperament allowed her to combine spiritual discernment with decisive leadership.

Esther - Gentle, poised, and wise. Her temperament gave her the grace to influence a king and save her people.

Paul - Relentless and uncompromising, able to endure hardship and establish doctrine with clarity.

Barnabas - Known as "the son of encouragement," his temperament made him the perfect bridge-builder between leaders and believers.

Each personality became a platform for God's purpose. None of them were asked to exchange their wiring for someone else's. Instead, God used their uniqueness to display His glory. The same is true for you. Whether you identify as a social introvert, a thinker, a dreamer, or a leader who thrives behind the scenes, your temperament is part of your assignment. When surrendered to God, it becomes an instrument for Kingdom impact. Comparison whispers, "I should be more like them." But calling declares, "I was designed for this."

Introversion as a Strategy; Not a Flaw

In our culture, extroversion is often misunderstood as always being loud, highly social, or constantly in the spotlight. But not all extroverts fit that picture. Some are naturally charismatic, while others are steady but energized by group interaction. What defines extroversion is not volume but the way a person recharges; they draw strength from being with people.

In the same way, introversion is often misrepresented as weakness; "too quiet," "too private," "not bold enough." Yet what defines an introvert is not shyness, but the need for solitude to refuel. When you see it through a Kingdom lens, introversion is not a limitation. It is a strategic design. God often works through what is hidden, reflective, and quiet to accomplish things that require discernment and depth.

1 Corinthians 1:27 (NKJV) says: "But God has chosen the foolish things of the world to put to shame the wise, and God has chosen the weak things of the world to put to shame the things which are mighty."

When you pause to process before acting, you are not falling behind; you are aligning yourself for wisdom. When you withdraw to regain strength, you are not retreating in fear; you are positioning yourself for clarity. Think of Joseph in Egypt. He wasn't the most visible presence in Pharaoh's court, but he was the most discerning. His ability to listen, interpret, and strategize quietly was the very gift that positioned him to save nations. His reflective temperament became the key to his influence.

The same is true for you. What others may interpret as hesitation, God sees as preparation. Introversion is not your barrier; it is your advantage.

Living From Identity in Christ

At the core of your personality and purpose is your identity in Christ. If you build your confidence on personality alone, you will always feel the pressure to measure yourself against others. But when your identity is anchored in who God says you are, your personality becomes a tool instead of a trap.

Galatians 2:20 (NKJV) declares: *"I have been crucified with Christ; it is no longer I who live, but Christ lives in me; and the life which I now live in the flesh I live by faith in the Son of God, who loved me and gave Himself for me."*

Your personality may influence how you lead, create, and connect, but it is not the source of your worth. Christ is. You are not valuable because you are quiet or bold, social, or reflective, strategic, or spontaneous. You are valuable because you are His. When you live from identity in Christ, your personality finds balance. Comparison loses its grip. You stop asking, "Am I enough?" and start declaring, "I am chosen, equipped, and secure in Christ."

Ephesians 2:10 (NLT) says: *"For we are God's masterpiece. He has created us anew in Christ Jesus, so we can do the good things He planned for us long ago."*

You are God's masterpiece. Your wiring, your rhythm, and your introversion are brushstrokes of His design. And when yielded to Him, they will always serve the greater purpose of your calling.

Reflection Questions

- How does knowing that purpose precedes personality change the way you see yourself?
- Which biblical figure's personality resonates most with your own journey, and why?
- In what areas have you been tempted to see your introversion as a weakness instead of a Kingdom strategy?

✎ Write your reflections below:

Prayers

Father, I thank You that my purpose was established before my personality was formed. You knew me before I was born, and every detail of my life is written in Your book. I rejoice that I am not an accident, but a part of Your divine plan.

Lord, forgive me for the times I compared myself to others or felt inadequate because of how I am wired. Teach me to see my design the way You see it, as intentional, strategic, and useful for Kingdom work. Help me to walk in confidence, knowing that my personality is a tool, not my identity, and that my true identity is as Your beloved child.

Give me wisdom to steward the strengths You placed within me. Where I have believed lies about myself, replace them with truth from Your Word. Remind me daily that my calling is greater than my limitations, and my purpose is fueled by Your Spirit.

In Jesus' name, Amen.

Declarations

- I decree and declare that I am first and foremost a child of God, chosen and deeply loved.
- I decree and declare that my purpose was set before the foundation of the world, and my personality was designed to align with that purpose.
- I decree and declare that I embrace my God-given design and reject comparison or self-doubt.
- I decree and declare that I will walk in wisdom, stewarding both my strengths and limitations for God's glory.
- I decree and declare that I am fully equipped to fulfill the assignment God has placed in my hands.

In Jesus' mighty and matchless name, Amen!

Chapter 3: Entrepreneurship as Kingdom Assignment

Outline

- Work as Worship (Genesis 2:15; Colossians 3:23)
- Business Beyond Profit: Kingdom Impact
- Entrepreneurship as Stewardship (Parable of the Talents, Matthew 25:14-30)
- Social Introverts in the Marketplace (your unique advantage)
- Building With Eternal Perspective

Work as Worship

Entrepreneurship is not just about building wealth or independence, in the Kingdom, it is about stewardship and worship. Work itself was God's idea long before sin entered the world.

"Then the Lord God took the man and put him in the garden of Eden to tend and keep it." - Genesis 2:15 (NKJV). Before Adam ever sinned, he was entrusted with responsibility. Work was not punishment; it was purpose. In the same way, entrepreneurship is not just business, it is an expression of worship when surrendered to God.

Colossians 3:23 (NKJV) says: "And whatever you do, do it heartily, as to the Lord and not to men." This means your business meetings, your strategic planning, your product launches, and even your quiet times of reflection are opportunities to glorify God.

When you see your business as worship, everything changes. No task is too small, and no assignment is too ordinary, because every part of it can honor the One who gave you the vision.

Business Beyond Profit: Kingdom Impact

The world often defines success in business by profit margins, market share, and visibility. But in the Kingdom, success is measured by impact, how much your work advances God's purposes on earth. Jesus said: *"But seek first the kingdom of God and His righteousness, and all these things shall be added to you."* - Matthew 6:33 (NKJV)

This verse doesn't dismiss profit. It reorders it. Profit is not the end goal but the byproduct of aligning your business with Kingdom priorities. When your vision is surrendered to God, your business becomes more than a way to earn, it becomes a channel for influence, transformation, and service. Think of Lydia, the seller of purple cloth in Acts 16. Her business gave her influence in the marketplace, but she also used her resources and her home to advance the gospel. She was not known only for her wealth but for her impact on the Kingdom.

For the social introvert entrepreneur, this truth is liberating. You don't need to strive for endless visibility or compete for attention. Your greatest impact may come through intentional, smaller circles where you pour into people deeply, create systems that serve with excellence, and release strategies that outlast you.

Profit sustains your business. But Kingdom impact sustains your legacy. Kingdom entrepreneurship asks a different question than the world. The world asks, "How much can I gain?" The Kingdom asks, "How much can I give, build, and multiply for God's glory?"

Proverbs 11:25 (NLT) says: *"The generous will prosper; those who refresh others will themselves be refreshed."* Profit in the Kingdom is not just for accumulation but for circulation. God blesses your business so that you can bless others, employees, clients, communities, and even nations.

In scripture, Boaz stands as an example of this principle. As a wealthy landowner, he didn't hoard his resources. Instead, he practiced generosity through gleaning laws and later acted as a kinsman-redeemer for Ruth (Ruth 4). His wealth was not only for personal gain but for restoration and legacy, a lineage that led to King David and ultimately to Christ.

In more recent history, we see men and women who embodied this Kingdom mindset. R.G. LeTourneau, one of the world's greatest inventors in heavy machinery, gave away 90% of his income to missions and Kingdom work, living on the remaining 10%. David Green, founder of Hobby Lobby, built his company on biblical principles, investing millions annually into Bibles, ministries, and global missions. Truett Cathy, the founder of Chick-fil-A, modeled stewardship by closing every restaurant on Sundays to honor God, sacrificing profit for obedience.

These stories remind us that true Kingdom entrepreneurs measure success not by profit margins alone but by eternal impact. For the social introvert entrepreneur, this perspective is powerful. You may not always be drawn to stages or spotlights, but you can shape history through faithfulness and generosity. Your ability to see beyond profit positions you to create sustainable impact that echoes into eternity.

Entrepreneurship as Stewardship

At its core, entrepreneurship in the Kingdom is not about ownership but stewardship. Everything you have, your gifts, your resources, your opportunities, ultimately belongs to God. You are not the source; you are the steward. Jesus taught this principle in the Parable of the Talents:

"For the kingdom of heaven is like a man traveling to a far country, who called his own servants and delivered his goods to them. And to one he gave five talents, to another two, and to another one, to each according to his own ability; and immediately he went on a journey." - Matthew 25:14-15 (NKJV)

The talents were not the servants' property. They were entrusted resources. The master expected them to multiply what was given, not hide it in fear. The servant who buried his talent was rebuked, while those who multiplied their talents were rewarded with even greater responsibility. This parable reminds us that God expects fruitfulness. He is not glorified when we bury our gifts out of fear, comparison, or self-doubt. He delights when we take what He has given, no matter how small it looks, and multiply it for His glory.

As a social introvert entrepreneur, this means your reflective nature is not an excuse to hide your gifts, but a grace to steward them wisely. God does not ask you to be someone else; He asks you to multiply what He has placed in your hands. Scripture gives us many pictures of faithful stewards who multiplied what God entrusted to them. Joseph managed Pharaoh's resources during famine with wisdom, saving nations from starvation. Daniel stewarded his influence in Babylon with integrity, standing firm in faith while serving with excellence in a foreign system. The Proverbs 31 woman stewarded her household and business dealings so well that her family and community were blessed by her diligence. In each case, stewardship went beyond possessions. It included wisdom, relationships, influence, and time. These servants of God understood that their lives were not their own.

We see this echoed in history as well. William Wilberforce stewarded his influence in politics to fight for the abolition of slavery. George Washington Carver stewarded his scientific discoveries to bless farmers and communities rather than hoarding them for personal gain. These were not simply acts of talent; they were acts of stewardship; using what God had placed in their hands for Kingdom impact.

The lesson is clear: stewardship is about multiplying for impact, not just managing for survival. It is about holding everything loosely, knowing it belongs to God, and being diligent to make it fruitful.

Social Introverts in the Marketplace

The marketplace often elevates speed, visibility, and constant activity. But Kingdom wisdom shows us that true influence often comes through strategy, patience, and timing. Social introverts thrive in this space because they carry a rhythm many overlooks, the ability to fully engage and then intentionally pause. This rhythm creates a unique business advantage. Social introverts can walk into a room and contribute meaningfully, but their real strength is in what happens afterward. They take the time to process, evaluate, and listen to God before making key decisions. In an age where many rush to respond, their delay is not weakness, it is discernment.

Nehemiah is an example of this strength in action. When the burden to rebuild Jerusalem's walls came upon him, he didn't announce it immediately. He spent days in prayer, seeking God's strategy. Then he inspected the ruins quietly at night before unveiling his plan. His ability to balance engagement with reflection positioned him to succeed where others had failed.

This same principle applies to business today. Many entrepreneurs chase trends or compete to be the loudest voice in the room. Social introverts take another path. They observe details others miss, build partnerships quietly but meaningfully, and design systems that last beyond the noise of the moment. Their advantage is not in competing with extroverted energy, but in walking faithfully in their own God-given rhythm.

Isaiah 28:16 (NLT) captures this steadiness: *"I lay a foundation in Zion, a stone that is tested and precious. Whoever believes need never be shaken."* Social introverts, rooted in Christ, embody this principle. They may not rush, but when they act, they do so with clarity, precision, and confidence.

Building With Eternal Perspective

Every entrepreneur builds something a business, a brand, a system, or a legacy. But the real question is: Will what you are building last into eternity?

Psalm 127:1 (NKJV) declares: *"Unless the Lord builds the house, they labor in vain who build it; unless the Lord guards the city, the watchman stays awake in vain."* Without God as the foundation, even the most impressive projects crumble. With Him, even ordinary work becomes eternal seed.

The Apostle Paul reminds us of this truth in *1 Corinthians 3:12-14 (NLT)*: *"Anyone who builds on that foundation may use a variety of materials - gold, silver, jewels, wood, hay, or straw. But on the judgment day, fire will reveal what kind of work each builder has done. The fire will show if a person's work has any value. If the work survives, that builder will receive a reward."*

This means entrepreneurship is never just about profit or influence. It is about partnering with God to create something that endures beyond your lifetime. Systems that bless communities. Ideas that open doors for the gospel. Businesses that model integrity in a corrupt world. These are the things that will be tested and rewarded eternally.

As a social introvert entrepreneur, you may already carry this eternal perspective. Your tendency to reflect, withdraw, and seek clarity often aligns with God's call to build slowly and intentionally. While others may rush to scale without a foundation, you have the grace to pause, seek God, and ensure that what you build carries His fingerprint.

Building With Eternal Perspective (Practical Application)

Building with eternity in mind means making choices that may not always make sense to the world but align with Kingdom values. It shifts the question from "What will bring me the fastest profit?" to "What will bring God the greatest glory?"

Here are some ways this eternal mindset shows up in entrepreneurship:

Integrity Over Compromise - Choosing honesty in contracts, finances, and practices even when cutting corners could save money. Eternal perspective recognizes that integrity leaves a testimony that profit alone cannot buy.

People Over Platform - Valuing employees, clients, and partners as people created in God's image rather than merely tools for success. Every interaction becomes a seed of the Kingdom.

Legacy Over Trend - Designing systems, products, or services that will last, rather than chasing what is popular or for the moment. Eternal builders think generationally, not temporarily.

Kingdom Over Self -Tithing, giving, and sowing into Kingdom work. Eternal perspective knows that true wealth is measured in lives impacted, not just numbers in an account.

Jesus said: *"Do not lay up for yourselves treasures on earth, where moth and rust destroy and where thieves break in and steal; but lay up for yourselves treasures in heaven... For where your treasure is, there your heart will be also." - Matthew 6:19-21 (NKJV)*

For the social introvert entrepreneur, this perspective is liberating. You don't have to fight for endless visibility or chase every new trend to prove your worth. Instead, you are free to build intentionally, guided by the Spirit, knowing that what you create has eternal weight.

Reflection Questions

- How do you see your business, career, or creative work as part of God's Kingdom assignment?
- Which example of a biblical entrepreneur (Joseph, Proverbs 31 woman, Paul, etc.) most inspires you, and why?
- Where do you sense God calling you to steward your influence or resources more intentionally for His glory?

✎ Write your reflections below:

Prayers

Father, I thank You that entrepreneurship is not simply business, but Kingdom assignment. You have entrusted me with gifts, skills, and opportunities that are meant to glorify You and serve others. Help me to see my work as worship, and my business as ministry.

Lord, I surrender every idea, every plan, and every resource back to You. Remove from me the pressure to compete or compare and instead let me build with prophetic precision and divine timing. Teach me to be faithful in little so that I may be trusted with much.

Holy Spirit, give me discernment in relationships, wisdom in decisions, and endurance in challenges. May my influence and resources be stewarded in a way that advances Your Kingdom and blesses generations to come.

In Jesus' name, Amen.

Declarations

- I decree and declare that my entrepreneurship is a Kingdom assignment, not just a personal ambition.
- I decree and declare that everything I build will glorify God and serve people with excellence.
- I decree and declare that I am a faithful steward of the resources, gifts, and opportunities God has entrusted to me.
- I decree and declare that I walk in prophetic precision and divine timing in every business decision.
- I decree and declare that my influence multiplies for Kingdom impact across nations and generations.
- I decree and declare that I am rooted in God's wisdom and radiant in His purpose as I carry out my assignment.

In Jesus' mighty and matchless name

Part Two: The 30-Day Devotional Journey

Section 1: Identity & Design

Day 1 - Fearfully & Wonderfully Made

Scripture:

"I will praise You, for I am fearfully and wonderfully made; marvelous are Your works, and that my soul knows very well." - Psalm 139:14 (NKJV)

Devotional

As a social introvert entrepreneur, it can be easy to question your design. Some days, you show up as the engaging conversationalist who draws people in. Other days, you long for quiet, and those around you may misinterpret your stillness. Society often pressures you to "pick a side," but God calls you to embrace the fullness of who He created you to be.

David's words in Psalm 139 are a reminder that your design was intentional. You were not an afterthought or a misfit in God's blueprint. Every detail of your wiring, your need for reflection, your bursts of social energy, your ability to both connect and withdraw, is part of a divine strategy. What others may misunderstand, heaven calls marvelous.

When you start from the truth that you are fearfully and wonderfully made, you stop striving to be someone else. Confidence no longer comes from comparison but from identity. And from that identity flows the creativity, discernment, and resilience needed to build businesses that reflect God's glory.

Reflection Prompts

- In what areas of life or business have you doubted the way God designed you?
- How can embracing your unique personality free you to build with greater confidence?

✎ Write your reflections below:

Prayer

Father, I thank You that I am fearfully and wonderfully made. Forgive me for the times I have doubted my design or wished to be someone else. Teach me to see myself through Your eyes and to walk in confidence as the person You created me to be. Let my identity in Christ become the foundation of everything I build. In Jesus' name, Amen.

Declarations

- ❖ I decree and declare that I am fearfully and wonderfully made by God.
- ❖ I decree and declare that my design is intentional and carries Kingdom purpose.
- ❖ I decree and declare that I embrace my identity in Christ with confidence and boldness.

Action Step

Take 5 minutes today to write down three qualities about yourself that reflect God's intentional design. Thank Him for each one and ask Him how He wants you to use them in your work this week.

Day 2 - Seasons of Silence & Speech

Scripture

"…a time to tear, and a time to sew; a time to keep silence, and a time to speak." - Ecclesiastes 3:7 (NKJV)

Devotional

As a social introvert, you live in the tension of two worlds: silence and speech. There are moments when your presence is loud with influence, and others when your quietness carries more power than words. The world often misunderstands this rhythm. People may expect you to always be "on," or they may question your confidence when you choose stillness. But Ecclesiastes reminds us that both silence and speech are part of God's divine timing.

Jesus modeled this balance perfectly. At times, He spoke with authority that left crowds astonished. At other times, He kept silent before His accusers, letting His restraint speak louder than any defense. Both were obedience. Both were power.

As an entrepreneur, knowing when to speak and when to remain silent is a Kingdom strategy. Silence can preserve wisdom until the right moment. Speech, when Spirit-led, can shift atmospheres, close deals, and unlock opportunities. The key is discernment, listening to the Spirit to know which season you are in. You don't have to defend yourself in every room, nor do you have to withdraw when God prompts you to speak. Your confidence rests not in people's expectations, but in God's timing.

Reflection Questions

- In what situations have you felt pressured to speak when silence was wiser?
- Where might God be prompting you to use your voice with boldness rather than holding back?

✎ Write your reflections below:

Prayer

Father, thank You for designing me with both the gift of silence and the power of speech. Teach me to discern Your timing in every situation. Help me to honor You when I speak and when I withhold words. Let my silence carry wisdom and my speech carry grace. May both bring glory to You and impact to the people I serve. In Jesus' name, Amen.

Declarations

- ❖ I decree and declare that I walk in discernment, knowing when to speak and when to keep silent.
- ❖ I decree and declare that my words are Spirit-led and carry power, wisdom, and grace.
- ❖ I decree and declare that my silence is not weakness but obedience that protects and preserves purpose.

Action Step

Today, before responding in a meeting, conversation, or decision, pause for 30 seconds to silently ask the Holy Spirit: "Is this a time to speak or a time to be silent?" Record what happens as you obey His prompting.

Day 3 - Jesus, Our Pattern of Balance

Scripture

"So, He Himself often withdrew into the wilderness and prayed." - Luke 5:16 (NKJV)

Devotional

Jesus is the perfect example of balance for the social introvert entrepreneur. He moved easily among crowds, teaching multitudes, healing the sick, and dining with sinners. Yet He was just as intentional about withdrawing into solitude with the Father. Both were essential. His public ministry was fueled by His private devotion.

As a social introvert, you may wrestle with feeling "too much" in one setting and "not enough" in another. But Jesus shows us that both engagement and withdrawal are holy when aligned with the Father's will. His pattern reminds us that you don't have to choose one over the other; you are called to embrace both.

In business and leadership, this rhythm is life-giving. There are moments when God will call you to step forward, present your ideas, and lead boldly. There are also moments when He will pull you into quiet, to pray, reset, and regain perspective. Both are part of Kingdom strategy.

The key is dependence on the Spirit. Balance is not about equal time in every space, but about alignment with God's assignment for each season. When you follow Jesus' pattern, your workflows from intimacy rather than exhaustion, and your influence grows from obedience rather than striving.

Reflection Questions

- Where do you struggle more, engaging others or withdrawing into solitude?
- How can following Jesus' rhythm help you lead and build with greater balance?

✎ Write your reflections below:

Prayer

Jesus, thank You for modeling the perfect balance between engagement and solitude. Teach me to follow Your example in my own life and work. When I am called to speak, help me to speak with boldness. When I am called to withdraw, help me to honor that time with You. Let every part of my rhythm reflect Your pattern and bring glory to the Father. Amen.

Declarations

- ❖ I decree and declare that Jesus is my pattern of balance in life, business, and leadership.
- ❖ I decree and declare that I embrace both solitude with God and engagement with people as part of my Kingdom assignment.
- ❖ I decree and declare that I live and build from intimacy with the Father, not from striving.

Action Step

Schedule 15 minutes today for solitude with God, even if your calendar is full. Use that time to breathe, pray, or journal. Ask Him how He wants to balance your "crowd moments" and your "quiet moments" this week.

Day 4 - The Gift of Stillness

Scripture

"Be still, and know that I am God; I will be exalted among the nations, I will be exalted in the earth!" - Psalm 46:10 (NKJV)

Devotional

Stillness is often mistaken for inactivity, but in the Kingdom it is power. The world equates influence with movement, productivity, and noise. Yet God invites His people into stillness; not to do less, but to trust more. In the pause, He speaks. In the quiet, He strengthens. In the waiting, He reveals Himself.

For the social introvert entrepreneur, stillness is both a necessity and a gift. Your rhythm naturally requires moments to withdraw, but stillness in God goes deeper than recharging energy. It becomes the place where strategies are birthed, clarity is sharpened, and your confidence is rooted not in what you do, but in who God is.

Moses encountered this truth at the Red Sea when God told him, "Stand still, and see the salvation of the Lord" (Exodus 14:13). In the moment of greatest pressure, God's answer was not frantic activity but trust. Likewise, in your business or leadership, there will be seasons when the Spirit's command is not "go" but "wait." The waiting is not wasted - it is preparation for breakthrough.

Reflection Questions

- When has stillness felt difficult for you in life or business?
- How can you reframe stillness as a place of power and preparation, not passivity?

✎ Write your reflections below:

Prayer

Father, thank You for the gift of stillness. Teach me to trust You in the pauses and to rest in Your presence without fear. Help me to see waiting not as wasted time, but as preparation for what You are building in and through me. In stillness, remind me that You are God, and that Your plans will not fail. In Jesus' name, Amen.

Declarations

- ❖ I decree and declare that stillness is a gift, not a weakness, in my journey with God.
- ❖ I decree and declare that in stillness, I receive wisdom, clarity, and renewed strength.
- ❖ I decree and declare that I will not fear waiting, for in waiting God is working.

Action Step

Set aside 10 minutes today to sit in silence before God, no agenda, no requests. Simply acknowledge His presence. Write down one truth about Him that becomes clearer in the stillness.

Day 5 - Purpose Precedes Personality

Scripture

"Your eyes saw my substance, being yet unformed. And in Your book, they all were written, the days fashioned for me, when as yet there were none of them." - Psalm 139:16 (NKJV)

Devotional

Before you were born, God already ordained your purpose. Your personality, your introversion, your rhythm of solitude and engagement, your temperament, was crafted to serve that purpose, not the other way around. Dr. Myles Munroe often taught that "Purpose is the original intent in the mind of the Creator." You are not an accident of temperament; you are an intentional design for Kingdom assignment.

As a social introvert entrepreneur, this truth sets you free from comparison. You don't have to strive to match another leader's energy or mimic their style. Your wiring was chosen because it perfectly fits the work God prepared for you to do. Moses doubted his speech, yet God called him as a deliverer. Peter was impulsive, yet God shaped him into a rock of the early church. Each personality was aligned with divine purpose.

The world tells you to shape your personality to succeed. The Kingdom tells you to root your identity in Christ and let your personality flow from your God-given assignment. When you build from purpose, personality becomes a tool, not a limitation.

Reflection Questions

- Where have you believed your personality disqualifies you from certain assignments?
- How does knowing your purpose precedes your personality change the way you see yourself in business and leadership?

✎ Write your reflections below:

Prayer

Lord, thank You that my purpose was written before I was born. I surrender my personality, my strengths, and my limitations into Your hands. Align every part of me with the assignment You have given. Free me from comparison and help me to see that my design is a perfect fit for my destiny. In Jesus' name, Amen.

Declarations

- ❖ I decree and declare that my purpose was established by God before I was formed.
- ❖ I decree and declare that my personality is a tool designed to fulfill divine assignment.
- ❖ I decree and declare that I will not compare myself to others but walk boldly in God's unique plan for me.

Action Step

Write down one area of your personality you have often seen as a weakness. Ask God to show you how He intends to use that very trait as a strength in fulfilling your purpose.

Day 6 - The Spirit of Boldness & Love

Scripture

"For God has not given us a spirit of fear, but of power and of love and of a sound mind." - 2 Timothy 1:7 (NKJV)

Devotional

Fear often whispers that you are not enough, not loud enough, not visible enough, not bold enough to lead or build. But God reminds us that fear is not His gift. Instead, He has given you the Spirit of power, love, and a sound mind.

As a social introvert entrepreneur, boldness does not always look like being the loudest voice in the room. Sometimes, it is the quiet confidence to step into spaces where others doubt you belong. Other times, it is the courage to stay true to your convictions when compromise seems easier. And always, it is balanced by love; the Kingdom boldness that uplifts, encourages, and serves.

Paul encouraged Timothy, a young leader who struggled with timidity, to remember the Spirit within him. In the same way, your strength is not drawn from personality but from the Holy Spirit dwelling in you. Boldness in business, in leadership, and in life is birthed not from striving but from surrender. When love and soundness of mind anchor your boldness, your influence becomes lasting and Spirit-led.

Reflection Questions

- Where has fear tried to hold you back from stepping fully into your assignment?
- How can you express boldness that is rooted in love rather than ego?

✎. Write your reflections below:

Prayer

Holy Spirit, thank You for filling me with power, love, and a sound mind. I reject fear and every lie that tells me I am not enough. Strengthen me to walk in confidence, wisdom, and compassion. Let my boldness be marked by love and let my leadership reflect Your Spirit in every space I enter. In Jesus' name, Amen.

Declarations

- ❖ I decree and declare that I reject the spirit of fear and walk in the Spirit God has given me.
- ❖ I decree and declare that I am bold, Spirit-filled, and grounded in love.
- ❖ I decree and declare that I carry the power, wisdom, and confidence to fulfill my Kingdom assignment.

Action Step

Take one small step today in an area where fear has held you back, make the call, submit the idea, apply to the school, start the conversation. Write down how the Spirit of boldness and love showed up in that moment.

Section 2: Grace for Both Worlds

Day 7 - Rest for the Weary

Scripture

"Come to Me, all you who labor and are heavy laden, and I will give you rest." - Matthew 11:28 (NKJV)

Devotional

The life of an entrepreneur can be exhausting. Deadlines, financial pressure, endless meetings, and the responsibility of leading others can weigh heavily. For the social introvert, the strain can be doubled: after engaging socially, you still need space to recharge. Without intentional rest, burnout becomes inevitable.

But Jesus makes a personal invitation: "Come to Me." He does not offer simply a pause from activity, but a rest that restores the soul. This rest is not laziness or neglect of responsibility; it is the deep exchange of weariness for His strength. It is laying down the weight you were never meant to carry and receiving the grace to continue.

Rest is a Kingdom strategy. In moments of weariness, you may feel the need to push harder, work longer, or prove yourself. But God says His yoke is easy and His burden is light. Rest is an act of faith, trusting that God will sustain your vision even when you step away from striving.

For the social introvert entrepreneur, rest looks like honoring your body's need for solitude, protecting your mental energy, and creating rhythms that keep you aligned with the Spirit. It is here, in rest, that fresh creativity is birthed and strength is renewed.

Reflection Questions

- What areas of your life or business feel the heaviest right now?
- How can you practice intentional rest this week as an act of faith?

✎ Write your reflections below:

Prayer

Father, thank You for inviting me into Your rest. I surrender my burdens, anxieties, and striving at Your feet. Teach me to walk in rhythms of grace that restore my soul and renew my strength. Help me to honor rest as a gift, not as a weakness, and to trust You to sustain the work You've given me. In Your name I pray, Amen.

Declarations

- ❖ I decree and declare that I accept the invitation of Jesus to rest in Him.
- ❖ I decree and declare that I release weariness and receive supernatural strength.
- ❖ I decree and declare that rest is a divine strategy in my life, and I will walk in it without fear.

Action Step

Set aside one block of time this week to rest intentionally, no work, no striving. Use that time to worship, journal, or simply sit with God. Notice how it impacts your clarity and peace.

Day 8 - The Ministry of Presence

Scripture

"The LORD your God is in your midst, the Mighty One, will save; He will rejoice over you with gladness, He will quiet you with His love, He will rejoice over you with singing." - Zephaniah 3:17 (NKJV)

Devotional

Presence carries power. God's presence transforms atmospheres, comforts hearts, and brings breakthrough. As His image-bearers, we too carry a ministry of presence. For the social introvert entrepreneur, this is often one of the greatest gifts you bring into relationships and work. You don't always need to say much or dominate a room, simply being there with authenticity, attentiveness, and Spirit-led peace makes an impact.

Think about Jesus. Crowds were drawn to Him not only because of His words, but because of His presence. Children wanted to be near Him. The sick longed to touch Him. The broken felt safe in His company. He carried the presence of the Father everywhere He went. In a noisy world, presence is rare. Entrepreneurs often feel pressure to constantly broadcast, market, and promote. Yet people remember less about what you said and more about how they felt in your presence. Was it hurried or peaceful? Distracted or attentive? Draining or refreshing?

Your ministry of presence becomes a testimony when you walk into rooms carrying the peace of Christ. Whether it's a boardroom, a networking event, or a coffee with one client, you represent the Kingdom by how you show up.

Reflection Questions

- When has someone's simple presence ministered to you more than their words?
- How can you intentionally carry God's presence into your business relationships this week?

✎ Write your reflections below:

Prayer

Father, thank You for always being present with me. Teach me to carry Your peace, joy, and love into every space I enter. Let my presence reflect Your presence so that others encounter You through me. May I be known not for noise, but for carrying the fragrance of Christ in my daily work. In Jesus' name, Amen.

Declarations

- ❖ I decree and declare that I carry the presence of God into every room I enter.
- ❖ I decree and declare that my presence brings peace, clarity, and encouragement to others.
- ❖ I decree and declare that my influence is rooted not in noise but in Spirit-filled authenticity.

Action Step

This week, choose one interaction, a meeting, call, or conversation, and intentionally practice presence. Slow down, listen fully, and invite the Holy Spirit to use your presence to minister beyond words.

Day 9 - Chosen for the Inner Circle

Scripture

"Then He appointed twelve, that they might be with Him and that He might send them out to preach: and to have power to heal sicknesses and to cast out demons. Simon, to whom He gave the name Peter; James the son of Zebedee and John the brother of James…" - Mark 3:14-16 (NKJV)

Devotional

Jesus ministered to multitudes, but He chose twelve to walk closely with Him. And even within the twelve, there were moments when He invited only Peter, James, and John into deeper encounters, such as the Mount of Transfiguration and the Garden of Gethsemane. This reveals a Kingdom principle: intimacy is selective. Not everyone can walk in your inner circle.

As a social introvert entrepreneur, this truth is freeing. You may sometimes feel guilty for not having a wide circle of friends or for preferring depth over breadth in relationships. But Jesus Himself modeled this. While He loved all, He invested deeply in a few. He built intimacy and trust in a smaller circle, and from there multiplied impact to the nations.

In your business, ministry, or leadership, God is not calling you to stretch yourself thin across endless relationships. He is calling you to steward the right connections, the people He assigns to your inner circle. These are the ones who sharpen your vision, pray with you, and walk alongside you in the weight of your calling.

Reflection Questions

- Who are the "inner circle" people God has already placed in your life?
- How can you be more intentional in nurturing those relationships?

✎ Write your reflections below:

Prayer

Lord Jesus, thank You for showing me that intimacy is not about numbers but about obedience. Help me to discern who belongs in my inner circle. Give me wisdom to steward those relationships well, and courage to release connections that drain rather than strengthen. May my closest relationships honor You and multiply Kingdom impact. Amen.

Declarations

- ❖ I decree and declare that I am free from the pressure to please everyone.
- ❖ I decree and declare that God is surrounding me with the right people for my assignment.
- ❖ I decree and declare that I will nurture my inner circle with prayer, trust, and intentionality.

Action Step

Identify one person in your inner circle who has been a gift to your journey. Take time this week to encourage them, with a prayer, a message, or a simple act of kindness, and thank God for their role in your life.

Day 10 - Authenticity Opens Doors

Scripture

"We have spoken openly to you; our heart is wide open." - 2 Corinthians 6:11 (NKJV)

Devotional

In business and in life, it is tempting to put on a mask, to perform, to adapt, to hide parts of yourself for the sake of acceptance. Yet in the Kingdom, authenticity is power. Paul reminds the Corinthians that he ministered with his heart wide open. His influence was not built on pretense but on honesty and transparency.

As a social introvert entrepreneur, you may sometimes feel the pull to overcompensate in order to appear "more extroverted" or to suppress your need for solitude, so you seem "more social." But doors that open through performance require you to keep performing. Doors that open through authenticity allow you to remain free.

Authenticity does not mean sharing everything with everyone. It means showing up consistently as the person God made you to be, without apology. When you walk in authenticity, you attract the right clients, partners, and opportunities, those aligned with your values and your purpose. God does not bless the version of you that you pretend to be. He blesses the person He created you to be.

Reflection Questions

- Where are you tempted to hide or alter parts of yourself to fit others' expectations?
- How might walking in authenticity create greater freedom in your business and relationships?

✎. Write your reflections below:

Prayer

Father, thank You for creating me with intention. Forgive me for the times I have hidden or altered myself out of fear. Give me courage to walk in authenticity and freedom, trusting that You open the right doors for me. May my life and work reflect honesty, integrity, and the uniqueness of Your design. In Jesus' name, Amen.

Declarations

- ❖ I decree and declare that I walk in authenticity and freedom, without fear of rejection.
- ❖ I decree and declare that the right doors open for me because I show up as who God created me to be.
- ❖ I decree and declare that my life and business reflect integrity, honesty, and Spirit-led confidence.

Action Step

Choose one situation this week where you will intentionally show up authentically, even if it feels risky. Pay attention to how others respond, and record how it feels to walk in that freedom.

Day 11 - In Quietness is Strength

Scripture

"In returning and rest you shall be saved; in quietness and confidence shall be your strength." - Isaiah 30:15 (NKJV)

Devotional

The world often equates strength with volume, visibility, and relentless activity. Yet God declares that true strength is found in quietness and confidence. Quietness is not weakness; it is stability, trust, and the refusal to be shaken by noise.

For the social introvert entrepreneur, this truth is liberating. You don't need to compete with the loudest voice in the room to carry authority. Authority comes from alignment with God. Confidence comes from knowing that your identity and assignment are secure in Him.

Quietness is not about passivity or avoidance; it is about rootedness. It is the posture of one who knows when to speak, when to listen, and when to let silence testify louder than words. In seasons of transition, negotiation, or leadership, quietness equips you to stand firm while others scramble.

Isaiah 30:15 reminds us that salvation and strength are not birthed in striving but in returning, returning to the presence of God, to His promises, and to His perspective. In quietness, you are re-centered in His truth. And from that place of confidence, you lead, create, and build with stability that cannot be shaken.

Reflection Questions

- Where have you felt pressured to prove your strength through noise or striving?
- How can you practice quietness as a spiritual discipline this week?

✏. Write your reflections below:

Prayer

Father, thank You for teaching me that quietness is not weakness but strength. Help me to trust You deeply enough to rest in silence when needed. Give me confidence that comes not from striving but from Your presence. May my quietness carry the testimony of faith, and my confidence reflect the strength of Christ in me. In Jesus' name, Amen.

Declarations

- ❖ I decree and declare that my strength is rooted in quietness and confidence in God.
- ❖ I decree and declare that I do not need noise or striving to prove my authority.
- ❖ I decree and declare that I stand firm, unshaken, because my trust is in the Lord.

Action Step

Set aside a moment of intentional quiet today, no phone, no music, no distractions. In that stillness, ask God to show you one area where He wants you to stop striving and start trusting.

Day 12 - God Rejoices Over You

Scripture

"The LORD your God is in your midst, the Mighty One, will save; He will rejoice over you with gladness, He will quiet you with His love, He will rejoice over you with singing." - Zephaniah 3:17 (NKJV)

Devotional

Too often, entrepreneurs measure their worth by productivity, profits, or recognition. But God's view of you is not based on what you do, it is anchored in who you are. Zephaniah 3:17 paints a breathtaking picture: the God of the universe delights in you, sings over you, and quiets you with His love.

As a social introvert, you may feel unseen or misunderstood in a world that celebrates constant visibility. Yet heaven declares that you are deeply loved and fully celebrated. God does not merely tolerate your design. He rejoices over it. Your personality, your rhythm of engagement and solitude, your unique wiring, all are part of His marvelous workmanship.

This truth is the antidote to striving. You are not building to earn His approval; you are building from His delight. When you understand that God rejoices over you, you stop hustling for validation and start creating from a place of freedom. His joy becomes your strength, and His love becomes your anchor.

Reflection Questions

- How does it change your perspective to know that God rejoices over you, not just tolerates you?
- Where have you been striving for validation that God has already given in His love?

✎. Write your reflections below:

Prayer

Father, thank You for rejoicing over me with gladness and quieting me with Your love. Forgive me for the times I've sought validation in achievements or approval from others. Help me to rest in the truth that I am celebrated by You. Let Your delight be the foundation of my confidence and the fuel for everything I build. In Jesus' name, Amen.

Declarations

- ❖ I decree and declare that I am deeply loved and fully celebrated by God.
- ❖ I decree and declare that His joy strengthens me, and His love anchors me.
- ❖ I decree and declare that I build from a place of divine approval, not human striving.

Action Step

Take five minutes today to thank God aloud for rejoicing over you. Write down one area of your personality or work where you've doubted His delight and replace it with the truth: "God rejoices over this part of me."

Section 3: Boldness in Business

Day 13 - Occupy Till I Come

Scripture

"So, he called ten of his servants, delivered to them ten minas, and said to them, 'Do business till I come.'" - Luke 19:13 (NKJV)

Devotional

In this parable, Jesus uses the language of stewardship and responsibility. The Master entrusts His servants with resources and gives them a clear instruction: "Do business till I come." This was not a suggestion but a command. It reminds us that entrepreneurship and work are not secular distractions but sacred assignments.

As a social introvert entrepreneur, this scripture speaks directly to your call. You have been given talents, ideas, and resources, not to bury in fear or hide behind timidity, but to multiply for Kingdom impact. To "occupy" means to manage, steward, and expand what God has entrusted until Christ returns.

Boldness in business, then, is not about ego or ambition. It is about obedience. The Master expects fruitfulness, not excuses. Playing small is not humility; it is disobedience when God has equipped you to multiply. Your design may not look like the world's version of leadership, but it is still powerful in His hands.

For example, even the writing of this book is an act of obedience, a way of "occupying" what God placed within me. The ideas, testimonies, and revelations He deposited were not meant to remain hidden in my journals. Putting them into this devotional is a way of multiplying what He gave, turning private encounters into public encouragement. This is also true for you: every act of obedience to steward what God entrusted, no matter how small, is a form of occupying until He comes.

This is what it means to occupy till He comes: to faithfully multiply what God has placed in your hands through obedience, rather than hiding it in fear, and to leave a testimony of stewardship that points back to the King.

Reflection Questions

- What "mina" (gift, resource, or opportunity) has God entrusted to you in this season?
- In what ways might you be burying what God asked you to multiply?

✎. Write your reflections below:

Prayer

Lord, thank You for entrusting me with talents and opportunities. Forgive me for the times I have buried them in fear. Teach me to occupy faithfully until You come, multiplying what You have placed in my hands. May my business, my writing, and my work reflect Kingdom stewardship and bring You glory. In Jesus' name, Amen.

Declarations

- ❖ I decree and declare that I will faithfully occupy until Christ returns.
- ❖ I decree and declare that I am a steward of Kingdom resources, not an owner.
- ❖ I decree and declare that I will multiply what God has entrusted, not bury it in fear

Action Step

Identify one "mina", a skill, connection, or resource, that you have been underusing. Take a practical step this week to activate it, whether by creating, investing, or reaching out.

Day 14 - Wisdom Builds the House

Scripture

"Through wisdom a house is built, and by understanding it is established; by knowledge the rooms are filled with all precious and pleasant riches." - Proverbs 24:3-4 (NKJV)

Devotional

Success in the Kingdom is not built on noise, charisma, or chance. It is built on wisdom. Scripture reminds us that wisdom is not optional; it is the foundation of building anything that lasts. A house, a business, a ministry, or even a life will crumble without it.

As a social introvert entrepreneur, this truth is both comforting and empowering. You may not always feel like the loudest or most visible in a room, but wisdom makes your voice weighty and your decisions enduring. Wisdom goes beyond intelligence; it is applied knowledge guided by the Spirit of God.

Solomon, the wisest king, understood this. When given the opportunity to ask for anything, he did not request riches, long life, or victory over enemies. Instead, he asked for wisdom to lead God's people (1 Kings 3:9-12). And because he sought wisdom first, everything else was added to him. His example reminds us that wisdom secures what wealth cannot.

At the same time, wisdom often comes in ways that challenge our logic. In the wilderness, God told Israel to gather only enough manna for each day. To them, storing more seemed wise, but God was teaching them daily dependence (Exodus 16:16-20). Wisdom is not just clever strategy; it is alignment with God's instruction, even when it feels counterintuitive.

Others may rush ahead, chasing trends, while you take time to listen, research, and discern. This isn't delay, it is strategy. When you build with wisdom, your "house", whether it is your company, your calling, or your influence, will not only stand but flourish. This is the strength of wisdom: it builds slowly but securely, establishing what will stand when everything else around you shakes.

Reflection Questions

- Where have you been tempted to build quickly instead of building wisely?
- How can you invite the Spirit of wisdom into your daily decision-making?

✎ Write your reflections below:

Prayer

Lord, I thank You that wisdom comes from You. Like Solomon, I ask for wisdom above all else. Keep me from relying on my own understanding or rushing ahead without discernment. Teach me to recognize Your instructions, even when they challenge my logic. May everything, I build be rooted in wisdom and bring glory to You. In Jesus' name, Amen.

Declarations

- ❖ I decree and declare that I build my life and work on the foundation of God's wisdom.
- ❖ I decree and declare that I will not rush ahead in my own understanding but wait for the Spirit's guidance.
- ❖ I decree and declare that what I build will endure because it is rooted in wisdom and truth.

Action Step

Before making your next major decision, pause to pray specifically for wisdom. Write down one insight or shift in perspective you receive, and act on it with confidence.

Day 15 - Do Business God's Way

Scripture

"The blessing of the LORD makes one rich, and He adds no sorrow with it." - Proverbs 10:22 (NKJV)

Devotional

The marketplace is filled with strategies, formulas, and shortcuts for success. Yet not all success is the same. The world's version often comes with hidden costs, compromise, burnout, or broken relationships. God's way of doing business is different: His blessing brings increase without sorrow attached.

As a social introvert entrepreneur, this truth is essential. You may not be drawn to the flashy methods of others, but you are called to something greater, Kingdom stewardship. Doing business God's way means walking in integrity when shortcuts seem easier, choosing peace over pressure, and allowing God's wisdom to order your steps.

Consider Daniel. Though he worked in Babylon, he refused to defile himself with the king's food (Daniel 1:8). His decision to honor God in his daily choices led to favor and promotion. He excelled in a secular system because he was rooted in God's way. Likewise, your business may operate in the world, but it does not have to operate like the world.

I've also learned this in my own journey. There were times when I wanted to accept projects or events simply because they looked good on the outside. For example, I agreed to lead a team for a co-laborer I deeply respected. While in Nigeria for a quick visit, I planned to quickly return to also attend their event in Dallas. But the Holy Spirit told me I wasn't allowed to go, that I had to stay in Nigeria until He released me. I knew it would look bad to others, even disappointing, but obedience mattered more than optics.

Not going for that event cost me a lot. People came against my reputation, lied on me, and even made-up false stories. Yet I would not have it any other way. Obedience to God's instruction is more valuable than the approval of man. Doing business God's way may cost your comfort or your image for a season, but it will always protect your destiny.

This is the essence of doing business God's way: obeying His voice even when the world doesn't understand, trusting His blessing above man's approval, and building with peace instead of pressure.

Reflection Questions

- Where have you been tempted to adopt the world's methods instead of waiting for God's way?
- How can you align your business decisions more fully with Kingdom principles?

✎ Write your reflections below:

Prayer

Father, thank You that Your blessing brings increase without sorrow. Teach me to do business Your way, rooted in integrity and guided by Your wisdom. Protect me from shortcuts that lead to compromise. Let everything, I build reflect Your Kingdom, carry Your peace, and shine with Your glory. In Jesus' name, Amen.

Declarations

- ❖ I decree and declare that I do business God's way, not the world's way.
- ❖ I decree and declare that the blessing of the Lord enriches me and adds no sorrow.
- ❖ I decree and declare that my work will be marked by peace, integrity, and Kingdom fruitfulness.

Action Step

Examine one area of your business or work this week. Ask yourself honestly: Am I doing this God's way or the world's way? Write down one shift you can make to bring it back into alignment with His principles.

Day 16 - Speaking with Grace & Truth

Scripture

"Let your speech always be with grace, seasoned with salt, that you may know how you ought to answer each one." - Colossians 4:6 (NKJV)

Devotional

Words carry weight. In business and leadership, what you say, and what you do not say, shapes trust, credibility, and influence. Scripture instructs us to speak with both grace and truth. Grace without truth can become flattery, while truth without grace can become harshness. The Spirit calls us to walk in both. Grace and truth are not opposites; they are a Kingdom partnership. Grace is not weakness, and truth is not cruelty. Together, they form the balance of Spirit-led authority.

Deborah in Judges 4-5 is a striking example. As a prophetess and judge, she spoke with authority that could not be ignored. She summoned Barak with a command from the Lord, declared God's strategy for battle, and led a nation into victory. Her words were strong and direct, yet they were rooted in God's truth and carried the grace of His leadership. She shows us that speaking with grace and truth is not about tone, but about obedience to God's word spoken in His Spirit.

As a social introvert entrepreneur, you may not speak often, or you may speak freely when you are in trusted spaces. Social introverts can be talkative, expressive, and engaging, yet still need to retreat for renewal. Speaking with grace and truth is not about speaking less or more, but about how you speak when God gives you a voice. Whether your words are few or many, they must be Spirit-governed, bold, truthful, and seasoned with grace.

Jesus modeled this balance perfectly. He spoke truth to the Pharisees without compromise, but He also spoke grace to the broken, the sinner, and the outcast. His words both confronted and healed. In your life and work, you will often be called to do the same, to speak truth in love, seasoned with grace, so that your words build rather than destroy.

There have been moments when the Spirit asked me to say "no" or deliver a difficult message, even when silence would have been easier or more politically convenient. At times, this cost me relationships or opportunities. Yet learning to speak with grace and truth has preserved my integrity and allowed my words to carry Kingdom influence.

Reflection Questions

- Where do you feel the tension between speaking boldly and speaking graciously?
- How can you invite the Holy Spirit to guide your words in business conversations?

✎ Write your reflections below:

Prayer

Lord, thank You for the mantle of Deborah, a voice of strength, authority, and obedience. Teach me to speak as she did: declaring truth without fear and carrying grace that brings freedom. Let my words reflect Your Spirit, build Your people, and establish Your Kingdom in every space I enter. In Jesus' name, Amen.

Declarations

- ❖ I decree and declare that I speak with Spirit-governed authority like Deborah.
- ❖ I decree and declare that my words are seasoned with grace and anchored in truth.
- ❖ I decree and declare that when I speak, heaven backs my voice with weight and clarity.

In Jesus' mighty and matchless name, Amen!

Action Step

Identify one area this week where you have been holding back your voice out of fear of how others may perceive you. Ask the Holy Spirit for both the timing and the words, then step forward in boldness to speak with grace and truth.

Day 17 - Faith Over Fear in Leadership

Scripture

"Have I not commanded you? Be strong and of good courage; do not be afraid, nor be dismayed, for the LORD your God is with you wherever you go." - Joshua 1:9 (NKJV)

Devotional

Leadership is never without risk. Decisions must be made, people must be guided, and outcomes are not always certain. Fear whispers that you are not enough, that failure is inevitable, or that others are better suited. Yet God's command to Joshua. repeated multiple times, was simple: "Be strong and courageous." Leadership in the Kingdom rests not on the absence of fear, but on the presence of faith.

Joshua stepped into leadership after Moses, one of the greatest leaders in Israel's history. From a human perspective, that was intimidating. Yet God reminded Joshua that the assignment was not about comparison but about obedience. The strength to lead came not from Joshua's personality but from God's presence.

As a social introvert entrepreneur, this truth is essential. you may be expressive and talkative at times or reserved and observant at others. Neither tendency disqualifies you from leadership. What matters is whether fear or faith governs your decisions. Social introverts often carry the gift of discernment, but fear can distort discernment into hesitation. Faith, however, transforms discernment into Spirit-led strategy.

This is the essence of faith over fear in leadership: not denying fear exists but refusing to let it dictate your steps. Faith is not the absence of trembling, it is the choice to obey God's command anyway, trusting His presence to back you up.

Reflection Questions

- Where has fear tried to silence your leadership voice?
- What step of faith is God calling you to take in leadership right now?

✎ Write your reflections below:

Prayer

Lord, thank You that You are with me wherever I go. Forgive me for the times I've let fear hold me back. Strengthen me to lead with courage, not because I am fearless, but because You are faithful. Teach me to walk by faith in every decision, knowing You go before me. In Jesus' name, Amen.

Declarations

- ❖ I decree and declare that I lead by faith, not by fear.
- ❖ I decree and declare that God's presence strengthens me to make bold decisions.
- ❖ I decree and declare that my leadership carries courage rooted in His Word.

In Jesus' mighty and matchless name, Amen!

Action Step

Write down one leadership or business decision you have delayed because of fear. Pray over it and take one faith-filled step toward action this week.

Day 18 - Diligence Brings Influence

Scripture

"Do you see a man who excels in his work? He will stand before kings; he will not stand before unknown men." - Proverbs 22:29 (NKJV)

Devotional

Influence in the Kingdom is not built on self-promotion or chasing platforms. It is established through diligence, the consistent, faithful work of showing up and excelling in what God has placed in your hands. Scripture promises that the diligent will eventually stand before kings. In other words, diligence attracts influence.

Joseph's life is a powerful example. Though betrayed, sold into slavery, and wrongfully imprisoned, he remained diligent in every assignment. As a servant in Potiphar's house, as a prisoner in the king's jail, and finally as governor over Egypt, Joseph's diligence distinguished him. Each stage prepared him for the next, until his diligence carried him into the palace where he stood before Pharaoh.

As a social introvert entrepreneur, diligence is often your hidden strength. You may not seek constant spotlight, but you thrive in building systems, cultivating consistency, and giving full attention to the work entrusted to you. While others may rely on charisma or loudness to get noticed, diligence allows your work to speak for you. Social introverts can be talkative and expressive in the right spaces, but what sustains influence long-term is not personality alone, it is faithfulness.

This is the truth: God does not reward hurried striving, but He does reward steady diligence. Influence gained by shortcuts quickly fades, but influence built by diligence endures and multiplies. Your diligence is not wasted; it is your seed for divine promotion.

Reflection Questions

- Where is God calling you to show greater diligence in this season?
- How has diligence already opened doors of influence in your life or work?

✏. Write your reflections below:

Prayer

Father, thank You for the reminder that diligence honors You and attracts influence. Strengthen me to remain faithful in the assignments You have given, even when no one is watching. May my diligence create open doors that bring glory to Your name and expand Your Kingdom. In Jesus' name, Amen.

Declarations

- ❖ I decree and declare that my diligence distinguishes me and makes room for divine influence.
- ❖ I decree and declare that I will excel in my work and stand before the opportunities God ordains.
- ❖ I decree and declare that my consistency will speak louder than my striving.

In Jesus' mighty and matchless name, Amen!

Action Step

Choose one area of your business or work where you've been inconsistent. Commit to showing up diligently this week, tracking your progress, and offering it as worship to God.

Section 4: Rest & Recharge

Day 19 - Abide in the Vine

Scripture

"I am the vine, you are the branches. He who abides in Me, and I in him, bears much fruit; for without Me you can do nothing." - John 15:5 (NKJV)

Devotional

True rest is not simply sleep or a vacation; it is abiding in Christ. Jesus reminds us that fruitfulness is not the result of endless striving but of remaining connected to Him, the true Vine. The branch does not produce fruit by effort; it produces fruit by connection.

As entrepreneurs, it is easy to confuse activity with productivity. You can attend meetings, launch projects, and engage with people, yet still feel empty and burned out if your soul is disconnected from Christ. Abiding is not inactivity; it is sustained activity rooted in His presence.

Consider Mary of Bethany. While Martha busied herself with service, Mary chose to sit at Jesus' feet (Luke 10:38-42). Her posture reminds us that abiding precedes doing. As a social introvert entrepreneur, you may already value solitude, but the goal is not just being alone, it is being with Him. Whether you are naturally talkative or reserved, the key is learning to recharge by drawing life from Christ, not from the applause of people or the pressure of performance.

This is the essence of abiding: to remain in continual fellowship with Jesus so that every part of your work and leadership flows out of His strength, not your own.

Reflection Questions

- What practices help you remain connected to Christ in your daily work?
- Where are you striving in your own strength instead of abiding in Him?

✎ Write your reflections below:

Prayer

Lord Jesus, thank You for being the true Vine. Forgive me for the times I have tried to produce fruit apart from You. Teach me to abide daily in Your presence so that my life and work reflect Your strength and not my striving. Let my business and leadership flow from the rest I find in You. In Jesus' name, Amen.

Declarations

- ❖ I decree and declare that I abide in Christ, and His life flows through me.
- ❖ I decree and declare that my fruitfulness comes from connection, not striving.
- ❖ I decree and declare that I will walk in rest, recharge, and renewal through Him.

In Jesus' mighty and matchless name, Amen!

Action Step

Block out 20 minutes today to simply sit with God, no phone, no agenda, no multitasking. Read John 15 slowly and let Him remind you that your fruitfulness flows from abiding.

Day 20 - Elijah by the Brook

Scripture

"Then the word of the LORD came to him, saying, 'Get away from here and turn eastward, and hide by the Brook Cherith, which flows into the Jordan. And it will be that you shall drink from the brook, and I have commanded the ravens to feed you there.'" - 1 Kings 17:2-4 (NKJV)

Devotional

Before Elijah confronted kings and called down fire from heaven, he first learned the discipline of rest and dependence by the brook. God commanded him to withdraw, to hide, and to be sustained supernaturally. Ravens brought food. The brook supplied water. His assignment did not begin with activity but with stillness, trust, and hidden preparation.

For the social introvert entrepreneur, the "brook" seasons are often necessary. These are the times when God intentionally pulls you away from the noise to restore your strength and prepare you for the next assignment. At the brook, striving ends and supernatural supply begins, teaching you that true success is rooted not in constant output but in God's faithfulness. Elijah's story reminds us that before great public assignments often come hidden seasons of stillness. God did not send him into battle immediately; He first sent him into hiding. In the same way, your strength does not flow only from moments of visible execution but also from the quiet places of refreshment with God. Even if you are naturally social or expressive at times, you still need the sacred rhythm of retreat where God recharges you for what lies ahead.

In real life, this might look like stepping away from nonstop projects to spend intentional time in prayer retreats, journaling with God, or creating boundaries that protect evenings for solitude. It may mean choosing a season of reduced visibility so that your spirit and creativity can be replenished. Sometimes the brook looks as practical as a quiet morning routine, a weekly Sabbath, or saying "no" to another demand on your calendar. For me, a brook season was staying in Nigeria for four months, no active service after a year of back-to-back travels and activities. Yet even there, my journaling led to multiple unplanned devotionals. It was proof that God can use the hidden season to refill me and still multiply what He had deposited. These rhythms become sacred places where God restores what constant motion has drained.

Rest is not wasted time; it is God's strategy for renewal. Elijah's time at Cherith strengthened him for the drought, the confrontation, and the revival that lay ahead. In the same way, your brook seasons are not a detour; they are preparation for greater influence.

Reflection Questions

- Where is God inviting you into a "brook season" of rest and renewal?
- How can you see times of hiddenness as preparation rather than delay?

✎. Write your reflections below:

Prayer

Father, thank You for the brook seasons in my life. Teach me to value rest, solitude, and hidden preparation as much as public fruitfulness. Help me to trust in Your supernatural supply and to release the pressure of constant striving. Open my eyes to recognize when I am in such a season, so I do not resist what You are doing but embrace it fully. May my time by the brook refresh me and prepare me for the assignments ahead. In Jesus' name, Amen.

Declarations

- ❖ I decree and declare that I will not despise the seasons of rest and hiddenness God calls me into.
- ❖ I decree and declare that I am sustained by God's supernatural supply, not by striving.
- ❖ I decree and declare that I emerge from my brook seasons with fresh vision and renewed strength.

In Jesus' mighty and matchless name, Amen!

Action Step

Schedule one "brook moment" this week, a block of time to disconnect from demands and simply rest with God. Treat it as an appointment with Him, not an interruption.

Day 21 - The Gift of Sleep & Renewal

Scripture

> "It is vain for you to rise up early, to sit up late, to eat the bread of sorrows; for so He gives His beloved sleep." - Psalm 127:2 (NKJV)

Devotional

Sleep is not a weakness; it is a gift from God. In a world that glorifies hustle and endless productivity, it can feel almost irresponsible to rest. Yet Psalm 127 reminds us that working without pause, rising early and staying up late in constant striving, leads only to emptiness. God, in His love, gives sleep as a form of renewal for His beloved.

For the social introvert entrepreneur, sleep is more than physical rest. It is a reminder that you are not holding the world together; God is. When you lay down at night, you surrender control and trust that He is working even as you sleep. Renewal happens in your body, your mind, and your spirit. Many breakthroughs come not in exhaustion, but after rest resets your clarity and strength.

There was a time in my life when I used to say, "I'll rest when I die." But that is not biblical. That mindset was fueled by striving and the world's idea of hustle, not by God's design. Rest is not laziness, it is obedience. Rest is a form of worship, an acknowledgment that God is God and I am not. When I choose to sleep, I am declaring that He is in control and that I trust Him to sustain me. Ignoring rest only led to weariness and burnout; while embracing it taught me that rest is sacred, a rhythm where God restores my body, renews my mind, and recharges my spirit.

In real life, this might look like choosing to honor a consistent bedtime even when work is unfinished, allowing your body to recover from constant travel, or building healthier rhythms that protect your sleep from late-night overthinking. For me, renewal often comes in surprising ways, nights of deep sleep after a draining season, or even short naps that reset my focus when I've been pouring out in meetings or creative work.

These simple acts of rest are God's way of recharging both body and vision.

Reflection Questions

- How have you viewed sleep in the past, as a gift or as a distraction from productivity?
- What changes could you make this week to honor sleep as part of your renewal rhythm?

✎ Write your reflections below:

Prayer

Father, thank You for the gift of sleep and the renewal it brings. Forgive me for the times I have treated rest as weakness or neglected the rhythms You designed for my health. Teach me to see sleep as an act of faith, trusting that You are at work even as I rest. Restore my body, mind, and spirit so that I rise each day refreshed to walk in Your assignment. In Jesus' name, Amen.

Declarations

- ❖ I decree and declare that I receive sleep as a gift from God, not a weakness.
- ❖ I decree and declare that my nights are filled with peace, rest, and renewal.
- ❖ I decree and declare that as I sleep, God restores my body, mind, and spirit for His purposes.

In Jesus' mighty and matchless name, Amen!

Action Step

Set a consistent bedtime for the next three nights. Treat it as a sacred appointment with God's gift of renewal. Journal afterward about how honoring rest affects your clarity and energy.

Day 22 - Peace That Guards You

Scripture

"Be anxious for nothing, but in everything by prayer and supplication, with thanksgiving, let your requests be made known to God; and the peace of God, which surpasses all understanding, will guard your hearts and minds through Christ Jesus." - Philippians 4:6-7 (NKJV)

Devotional

Peace is more than the absence of conflict; it is the active presence of God guarding your inner life. Paul describes it as a peace that surpasses understanding, one that protects your heart and mind like a shield. For the social introvert entrepreneur, this truth is essential. you may carry the quiet weight of responsibilities, decisions, and the energy that comes with balancing both solitude and social spaces. Without the peace of God, anxiety quickly sets in.

Peace is not something you manufacture; it is something you receive. It comes when prayer replaces worry, when gratitude quiets fear, and when trust in God silences the inner noise. The peace of God does not always change circumstances immediately, but it changes you so you can endure them with clarity and strength.

There was a time in my life when I lived with constant inner noise, replaying conversations, overthinking decisions, and worrying about outcomes. But when I began to practice surrender through prayer, I discovered that peace itself was a weapon. It was not passive, but active. I realized that when I allowed God's peace to guard me, I could step into meetings, lead projects, or face uncertainties with a calm that defied logic. For me, peace became proof that God was not only present but actively fighting for my stability.

In real life, this might look like pausing before an overwhelming decision to breathe a prayer instead of spiraling into worry or writing down your anxieties and replacing each one with a declaration of trust in God. For me, it often looks like worship in the middle of pressure, turning on a song that shifts the atmosphere, journaling scripture over my fears, or choosing to thank God when I feel least in control. These simple acts allow peace to do its guarding work in my heart and mind.

Reflection Questions

- What situations most often steal your peace?
- How can you invite God's peace to guard your heart this week instead of carrying the weight yourself?

✎ Write your reflections below:

Prayer

Father, thank You for Your peace that surpasses understanding. Forgive me for the times I have chosen anxiety over trust. Help me to surrender my worries in prayer and to cultivate gratitude in every season. Let Your peace guard my heart and mind, shielding me from fear and confusion. Teach me to recognize when I am stepping out of peace and draw me back into Your presence. In Jesus' name, Amen.

Declarations

- ❖ I decree and declare that the peace of God guards my heart and mind through Christ Jesus.
- ❖ I decree and declare that I will not be ruled by anxiety, but by prayer, trust, and thanksgiving.
- ❖ I decree and declare that peace is my portion, my shield, and my testimony in every season.

Action Step

Write down three anxieties that have been heavy on your heart. One by one, release them to God in prayer, and then write a statement of gratitude that affirms your trust in Him.

Day 23 - Strength in Stillness

Scripture

"In returning and rest you shall be saved; in quietness and confidence shall be your strength." - Isaiah 30:15 (NKJV)

Devotional

Stillness is not inactivity; it is a posture of strength rooted in trust. The world equates strength with motion, hustle, and noise, but God redefines it as quiet confidence. True power comes when you are anchored in Him, even while everything around you seem uncertain.

For the social introvert entrepreneur, stillness is not always easy. You live in the tension of solitude and social engagement. You may even feel pressure to "prove yourself" by speaking up more, working longer, or staying constantly visible. But God reminds us that strength is not found in endless activity; it is found in quietness and returning to Him.

There was a season in my life when I learned this the hard way. I thought that if I just pushed harder, stayed longer in meetings, or accepted every opportunity, I would gain strength and success. Instead, I ended up depleted. It was only when I slowed down and embraced stillness with God that I discovered my clarity returned and my spirit was strengthened. The strength I was striving for came not from doing more but from surrendering more.

In real life, this might look like stepping out of a crowded networking event to take five minutes alone with God, closing your laptop earlier to pray instead of overworking, or simply sitting quietly with Scripture before making a big decision. For me, stillness often looks like journaling in silence after a long day or taking a quiet walk to clear my mind. These are not wasted moments; they are holy exchanges where God fills what noise has drained.

Reflection Questions

- Where have you confused busyness with strength?
- How can you intentionally embrace stillness this week as a way to renew your confidence in God?

✎ Write your reflections below:

Prayer

Lord, thank You for reminding me that strength is found in stillness with You. Forgive me for the times I have chased strength through striving and noise. Teach me to pause, to return, and to rest in You. Help me to recognize that stillness is not weakness but a place where confidence is renewed. In Jesus' name, Amen.

Declarations

- ❖ I decree and declare that my strength is rooted in stillness and confidence in God.
- ❖ I decree and declare that I am not driven by busyness but led by the Spirit into rest and clarity.
- ❖ I decree and declare that quietness with God equips me with supernatural strength for every assignment.

In Jesus' mighty and matchless name, Amen!

Action Step

Choose one area of your schedule this week to pause intentionally. Replace that time with five to ten minutes of stillness in God's presence. Write down how your confidence and clarity shift afterward.

Day 24 - The Shepherd Restores My Soul

Scripture

"He makes me to lie down in green pastures; He leads me beside the still waters. He restores my soul; He leads me in the paths of righteousness for His name's sake." - Psalm 23:2-3 (NKJV)

Devotional

David's words in Psalm 23 remind us that restoration is not something we manufacture; it is something the Shepherd gives. Just as sheep cannot find green pastures or still waters on their own, we cannot truly restore our own souls apart from Him. It is His leading, His care, and His presence that bring renewal.

For the social introvert entrepreneur, restoration is often needed after seasons of pouring out, leading, or navigating complex assignments. You may carry unseen emotional and spiritual weights even when you appear calm to others. The Shepherd sees those hidden burdens and leads you into places of refreshing.

There was a time in my journey when I felt drained from constant giving, pouring into events, teams, and projects without pausing long enough to be replenished. It was in those moments that God reminded me I am not the shepherd, He is. My role is not to keep myself together but to follow His leading into the still waters of His presence. Even when I resisted slowing down, He gently brought me back to prayer, worship, and quiet spaces where He could heal and renew me.

In real life, this might look like taking intentional breaks to worship when you feel empty, allowing Scripture to wash over you before you make another decision, or choosing to spend time outdoors as a way of meeting God in His creation. For me, restoration has often come in unexpected places, through writing devotionals in my journal, through stillness after travel, or through simple worship songs that reset my heart. These become the green pastures and still waters where my soul is restored.

Reflection Questions

- What drains your soul the most in this season?
- How is the Shepherd inviting you to green pastures and still waters right now?

✎. Write your reflections below:

Prayer

Lord, thank You for being my Shepherd who restores my soul. Forgive me for trying to carry weights I was never meant to bear. Lead me to the green pastures and still waters of Your presence. Restore my soul, renew my strength, and refresh my spirit so I can continue walking in righteousness for Your name's sake. In Jesus' name, Amen.

Declarations

- ❖ I decree and declare that the Lord is my Shepherd and He restores my soul daily.
- ❖ I decree and declare that I receive His leading into green pastures and still waters.
- ❖ I decree and declare that I walk in renewed strength, refreshed and sustained by His presence.

In Jesus' mighty and matchless name, Amen!

Action Step

Take 20 minutes this week to do something that restores your soul, whether worship, prayer, journaling, or walking in nature. Invite the Shepherd to meet you there and to fill you again.

Section 5: Community & Boundaries

Day 25 - Iron Sharpens Iron

Scripture

"As iron sharpens iron, so a man sharpens the countenance of his friend." —
Proverbs 27:17 (NKJV)

Devotional

No one is called to walk alone. While solitude is a gift, God also designed us to grow through community. Proverbs 27:17 reminds us that just as iron sharpens iron, people sharpen one another. Growth, accountability, and encouragement happen most powerfully in relationships.

For the social introvert entrepreneur, this truth can feel both challenging and freeing. You thrive in meaningful one-on-one connections but may hesitate in larger group settings. The beauty of God's design is that sharpening does not require the crowd; it often happens in small circles of trust. A single Spirit-led relationship can provide more growth than endless shallow interactions.

There was a time when I preferred to withdraw completely, thinking that solitude alone was enough for my growth. But God began to show me that without others speaking into my life, I was missing dimensions of wisdom and accountability. In moments when I wanted to stay hidden, He strategically placed voices that sharpened me, challenged me, and encouraged me forward. That sharpening wasn't always comfortable, but it was necessary for my assignment.

In real life, this might look like letting a friend speak truth into your blind spots, surrounding yourself with peers who challenge your excellence, or opening up to a trusted friend when you would rather remain silent. For me, sharpening has often come in conversations where someone asked the hard questions I avoided, or when a peer's encouragement gave me the courage to keep going. God uses people to refine us, just as He uses us to refine others.

Reflection Questions

- Who has God used to sharpen you in this season, and how have they impacted your growth?
- Who might God be calling you to sharpen through encouragement, wisdom, or accountability?

✏. Write your reflections below:

Prayer

Lord, thank You for the gift of community. Forgive me for the times I have resisted sharpening because it felt uncomfortable. Surround me with people who refine my faith, challenge my growth, and encourage my calling. And help me to be the same for others — a voice that sharpens and strengthens them in love. In Jesus' name, Amen.

Declarations

- ❖ I decree and declare that I embrace Kingdom relationships that sharpen and strengthen me.
- ❖ I decree and declare that I will not resist sharpening, even when it feels uncomfortable.
- ❖ I decree and declare that I am also a vessel God uses to sharpen others with wisdom and encouragement.

In Jesus' mighty and matchless name, Amen!

Action Step

Reach out to one person who has sharpened you in this season. Thank them for their role in your life and ask how you can also encourage or support them.

Day 26 - Guard Your Heart

Scripture

"Keep your heart with all diligence, for out of it spring the issues of life." - Proverbs 4:23 (NKJV)

Devotional

The heart is the wellspring of life. Every decision, every word, every vision you pursue flows from what is stored there. This is why Solomon urges us to guard it diligently. To guard your heart does not mean building walls of isolation; it means setting boundaries that protect your spirit, your values, and your intimacy with God.

For the social introvert entrepreneur, guarding the heart is especially important. Because you thrive in meaningful, deep connections, you may also be more vulnerable to disappointment, discouragement, or misplaced trust. Without healthy boundaries, your energy and focus can be drained by people or environments that do not align with your assignment.

There was a time when I allowed access to too many voices, thinking that being open meant being loving. But I quickly learned that not every voice deserved influence in my life. Guarding my heart meant learning to say "no" without guilt and protecting the space where God speaks to me. Boundaries did not make me unkind; they made me effective.

This may look like limiting time with people who constantly drain you, resisting the pressure to say "yes" to every request, or creating rhythms that keep your devotion to God first. For me, guarding my heart has looked like being selective about who I allow into my inner circle, and being intentional about filling my heart with Scripture and worship so that what flows out of me is life-giving.

Reflection Questions

- What boundaries do you need to put in place to better guard your heart?
- Are there voices or influences in your life that you need to limit in this season?

✎ Write your reflections below:

Prayer

Lord, thank You for reminding me that my heart is the wellspring of life. Forgive me for the times I have allowed wrong influences to shape my spirit. Teach me to guard my heart with wisdom and love. Help me to set boundaries that protect my intimacy with You and to fill my heart with what is pure, true, and life-giving. In Jesus' name, Amen.

Declarations

- ❖ I decree and declare that I guard my heart diligently, for it is the wellspring of life.
- ❖ I decree and declare that I set healthy boundaries without guilt or fear.
- ❖ I decree and declare that my heart is filled with God's truth, love, and wisdom.

In Jesus' mighty and matchless name, Amen!

Action Step

Write down one boundary you need to strengthen in this season. Commit it to prayer and take one practical step to implement it this week.

Day 27 - The Body Needs Every Part

Scripture

"For as the body is one and has many members, but all the members of that one body, being many, are one body, so also is Christ." - 1 Corinthians 12:12 (NKJV)

Devotional

God designed His Kingdom like a body, diverse parts working together in unity. Each member is different, but each one is necessary. Paul reminds us that no part can say to another, "I don't need you." In the same way, you are needed. Your personality, gifts, and calling have a place in the body of Christ and in the marketplace.

For the social introvert entrepreneur, this truth brings balance. You may sometimes feel overlooked because people assume passion and expressiveness only belong to extroverts. But your contribution carries weight. Your ability to be both relational and reflective, both expressive in leadership and intentional in retreat, is important to the Kingdom's advancement.

There was a season when I wondered if my passionate leadership style, sometimes bold, expressive, even loud when stirred, truly fit in spaces dominated by different personalities. But God reminded me that the body needs balance, eyes cannot say to the hands, "I don't need you." In fact, the parts that seem less visible are often the most essential. That revelation freed me to walk confidently in my role without apology, knowing that passion and introversion can coexist as part of God's intentional design.

This may look like collaborating with others whose strengths complement yours, celebrating gifts that are different from your own, or stepping fully into your lane without comparison. For me, it has looked like learning to honor both reserved introverted, and extroverted leaders while also valuing my own social introvert strengths, knowing all are needed for God's assignments to flourish.

Reflection Questions

- Where have you compared your role to someone else's instead of embracing your own part in the body?
- Who in your life or work can you celebrate this week for the unique gift they carry?

✎. Write your reflections below:

Prayer

Lord, thank You that I am a important part of Your body. Forgive me for the times I have compared myself or dismissed the value of my design. Help me to walk confidently in my calling while also honoring the gifts of others. Teach me to see every person, including myself, as necessary for the work of the Kingdom. In Jesus' name, Amen.

Declarations

- ❖ I decree and declare that I am a vital and necessary part of the body of Christ.
- ❖ I decree and declare that I will not compare myself to others but embrace my unique role.
- ❖ I decree and declare that I celebrate and honor the gifts of those God has placed around me.

In Jesus' mighty and matchless name, Amen!

Action Step

Write a note, message, or prayer of encouragement to someone whose gift you've overlooked. Let them know that you value their part in the body and thank God for them.

Section 6: Prophetic Precision & Vision

Day 28 - Write the Vision

Scripture

"Then the LORD answered me and said: 'Write the vision and make it plain on tablets, that he may run who reads it.'" - Habakkuk 2:2 (NKJV)

Devotional

Vision is a Kingdom principle. God gives His people dreams, assignments, and strategies, but He also commands us to write them down. Writing the vision makes it tangible, transferable, and actionable. What remains only in your head stays vague; what you write becomes a roadmap for yourself and for those who will run with you.

For the social introvert entrepreneur, writing is often a strength. Processing on paper brings clarity that conversations alone cannot. Journals, notes, and written strategies become places where God downloads revelation and direction. Writing the vision is not just organization, it is obedience.

There was a season when I had countless ideas swirling in my mind but no clarity on how to move forward. When I began to journal and write them down, the fog lifted. Later, some of those journal entries became devotionals and strategies I never planned but God birthed through writing. The simple act of recording vision created space for God to expand it.

This may look like journaling your prayers, creating a vision board with scriptures, writing down the open and close visions (dreams) you had, drafting business strategies that reflect Kingdom values, or writing down personal promises God has spoken to you. For me, it has meant treating my journals not just as private thoughts but as sacred spaces where God's vision becomes plain.

Reflection Questions

- What vision has God placed in your heart that you still need to write down?
- How could writing your vision help others run with it?

✎. Write your reflections below:

Prayer

Lord, thank You for giving me vision and purpose. Forgive me for the times I've kept Your instructions only in my head without writing them. Teach me to steward revelation with obedience and clarity. As I write the vision, make it plain so that others may run with it. Let my written words carry eternal impact for Your Kingdom. In Jesus' name, Amen.

Declarations

- ❖ I decree and declare that I write the vision God has entrusted to me with clarity and obedience.
- ❖ I decree and declare that what I record in faith will guide not only me but also those God has called to run with me.
- ❖ I decree and declare that my journals, strategies, and written plans are sacred tools for Kingdom advancement.

In Jesus' mighty and matchless name, Amen!

Action Step

Set aside 30 minutes this week to write one vision God has placed on your heart. Don't worry about perfection, just get it on paper. Then pray over it and ask God for the next step.

Day 29 - Times & Seasons

Scripture

"To everything there is a season, a time for every purpose under heaven." - Ecclesiastes 3:1 (NKJV)

Devotional

God is a God of timing. Every purpose under heaven is tied to a season, and wisdom comes from discerning the right time to act. Moving too early can cause frustration; moving too late can mean missed opportunities. The social introvert entrepreneur must learn to build not only with vision but also with prophetic sensitivity to times and seasons.

Discernment is important. Not every good idea is a "now" idea. Some visions need incubation. Others require preparation. Still others are released suddenly, demanding obedience without delay. Learning to move with God's timing protects you from burnout, wasted effort, and premature exposure.

There have been times when God instructed me to register businesses but made it clear they were not to be launched yet. He had me set them up legally and structurally but told me to wait until the appointed season to make them functional. Those experiences taught me that obedience is not always about immediate action; sometimes it is about preparation and patience. Trusting God's timing has reminded me that He knows when a vision will flourish, and my role is to follow His lead rather than rush ahead.

This may look like praying before saying "yes" to a new venture, fasting to discern timing, or journaling until God confirms His release. For me, it has looked like shelving ideas until the Spirit said "now", and when that moment came, doors opened effortlessly. Trusting His timing meant less striving and more fruitfulness.

Reflection Questions

- Where have you felt pressure to move outside of God's timing?
- What spiritual practices help you discern the difference between "now" and "not yet"?

✎ Write your reflections below:

Prayer

Father, thank You for being the God of times and seasons. Forgive me for the moments I have rushed ahead or lagged behind. Teach me to discern the season I am in and to move in step with Your Spirit. Give me wisdom to wait when it is not time, and boldness to act when You say "go." In Jesus' name, Amen.

Declarations

- ❖ I decree and declare that I walk in God's timing and not the pressure of people.
- ❖ I decree and declare that I discern the times and seasons of my assignment with clarity.
- ❖ I decree and declare that I move when God says move, and I rest when He says wait.

In Jesus' mighty and matchless name, Amen!

Action Step

Take one project, idea, or opportunity currently on your heart. Bring it before God in prayer this week and ask Him clearly: "Is this the time?" Write down any confirmations, impressions, or instructions you sense.

Day 30 - Finish Strong

Scripture

"I have fought the good fight, I have finished the race, I have kept the faith." - 2 Timothy 4:7 (NKJV)

Devotional

Finishing is as important as starting. Paul's words remind us that the measure of faithfulness is not in how loudly we begin, but in how steadily we endure to the end. The Kingdom does not celebrate half-built towers or abandoned assignments; it honors those who complete what God entrusted.

For the social introvert entrepreneur, this truth carries weight. You may start projects full of clarity and passion but find yourself drained by the demands of people, the pace of growth, or the hidden battles of the journey. Yet God's grace is not just for beginnings; it is for endurance. The same God who called you equips you to finish strong.

In my own journey, I've learned that finishing well often means leaning on God's strength when mine is gone. There have been times I wanted to pause permanently or step away, but God reminded me that what He starts, He sustains. Even when momentum feels low, finishing the assignment, whether a devotional, a business, or a project, becomes a testimony of His faithfulness. Passion may launch you, but persistence and obedience carry you to the end.

This may look like breaking large goals into smaller steps, so you don't lose focus, surrounding yourself with people who hold you accountable, or revisiting the vision God gave you when discouragement tries to blur it. For me, finishing strong has often meant going back to my journals, rereading what God first said, and allowing that original word to fuel me to completion.

Reflection Questions

- Where have you started something but felt tempted to stop halfway?
- What does "finishing strong" look like for you in this current season?

✎ Write your reflections below:

Prayer

Lord, thank You for the grace to finish strong. Forgive me for the times I have grown weary or tempted to abandon the assignment. Strengthen my hands and steady my heart to complete what You've entrusted to me. May my life be a testimony of faithfulness from start to finish, bringing glory to Your name. In Jesus' name, Amen.

Declarations

- ❖ I decree and declare that I finish the race God has set before me with endurance and joy.
- ❖ I decree and declare that I will not abandon what God has entrusted but complete it with excellence.
- ❖ I decree and declare that my life is marked by faithfulness, persistence, and strength to the end.

In Jesus' mighty and matchless name, Amen!

Action Step

Identify one unfinished project, vision, or assignment God has placed in your hands. Commit to taking one step this week toward completing it, no matter how small.

Go and Shine

Beloved, if you've walked through these pages, you've just completed a 30-day journey of discovery, reflection, and strengthening in God. That is no small thing. Every scripture read, every prayer whispered, every declaration made has been a seed planted in your spirit. Seeds may start small, but they carry the power of a forest within them.

As a social introvert entrepreneur, you now know that your design is not an obstacle, it is an intentional gift from God. The balance of solitude and connection, the rhythm of passion and rest, the ability to see deeply and build steadily, all of this was placed in you by a wise Creator who knew exactly what your generation would need.

This devotional was not just about insights for 30 days. It was about giving you tools, scriptures, and rhythms you can return to for the rest of your life. When you feel drained, revisit Rest for the Weary. When you question your personality, reread Purpose Precedes Personality. When you feel pressure to rush, go back to Times & Seasons. These words will meet you repeatedly because they are anchored in the living Word of God.

For me, writing this was also a journey of obedience, a form of "occupying" until He comes. Some of these devotionals were birthed in seasons of stillness, hidden journaling, or unexpected pauses. They are my testimony that God uses even the quietest places to produce fruit that lasts.

My prayer is that as you continue forward, you will finish strong. Not in striving, but in grace. Not in comparison, but in confidence. Not in fear, but in faith. And when others look at your life and your work, may they see more than an entrepreneur, may they see a son or daughter of the King, faithfully stewarding what has been entrusted. A king and a Priest.

You were not designed to fade into the background. You were designed to shine with a unique light, rooted and radiant, for the glory of God.

Prayer for You

Father, I lift up every reader of this devotional. May the seeds sown over these 30+ days take deep root in their hearts and bear fruit that remains, fruit that testifies of Your faithfulness and draws them closer to Your purpose. Let their lives reflect Your wisdom in every decision, let their businesses carry Your excellence in every detail, and let their voices shine with Your light wherever You have called them. Surround them with Your peace that quiets every anxious thought and strengthen them in their journey, so they never walk alone.

Lord, let Your presence steady them, Your word anchor them, and Your Spirit whisper direction when they need clarity. Align them with the right people, open the right doors, and close every door that leads them away from Your perfect will. Renew their courage, refresh their creativity, and breathe divine confidence into their calling. Let their steps be ordered, their hearts be assured, and their hands be empowered to build what You've placed within them.

I declare that they will finish strong, not by striving, but by grace. They will rise, move forward, and shine; rooted in Your love and radiant with Your glory. In Jesus' name, Amen.

Personal Notes (Your Journal Entry)

"The LORD will perfect that which concerns me;

Your mercy, O LORD, endures forever."

- Psalm 138:8 (NKJV)

THANK YOU JESUS